REST APIs with Django

Build powerful web APIs with Python and Django

William S. Vincent

REST APIs with Django

Build powerful web APIs with Python and Django

William S. Vincent

ISBN 9781983029981

© 2018 William S. Vincent

Also By William S. Vincent

Django for Beginners

Contents

Introduction   1
   Prerequisites   1
   Why APIs   2
   Django REST Framework   4
   Why this book   4
   Conclusion   5

Chapter 1: Web APIs   7
   World Wide Web   7
   URLs   8
   Internet Protocol Suite   9
   HTTP Verbs   10
   Endpoints   11
   HTTP   12
   Status Codes   15
   Statelessness   16
   REST   17
   Conclusion   17

Chapter 2: Library Website and API   19
   Traditional Django   19
   First app   23
   Models   26

CONTENTS

    Admin   27

    Views   31

    URLs   32

    Webpage   36

    Django REST Framework   36

    URLs   39

    Views   40

    Serializers   41

    cURL   42

    Browsable API   44

    Conclusion   45

Chapter 3: Todo API   **47**

    Initial Set Up   47

    Models   50

    Django REST Framework   54

    URLs   56

    Serializers   57

    Views   59

    Consuming the API   60

    Browsable API   61

    CORS   64

    Conclusion   66

Chapter 4: Todo React Front-end   **69**

    Install Node   69

    Install React   71

    Mock data   73

    Django REST Framework + React   78

    Conclusion   81

Chapter 5: Blog API — 83

    Initial Set Up — 83

    Model — 84

    Tests — 89

    Django REST Framework — 91

    URLs — 93

    Serializers — 94

    Views — 96

    Browsable API — 97

    Conclusion — 101

Chapter 6: Permissions — 103

    Create a new user — 103

    Add log in to the browsable API — 106

    AllowAny — 111

    View-Level Permissions — 113

    Project-Level Permissions — 115

    Custom permissions — 117

    Conclusion — 122

Chapter 7: User Authentication — 123

    Basic Authentication — 123

    Session Authentication — 125

    Token Authentication — 127

    Default Authentication — 129

    Implementing token authentication — 130

    Endpoints — 134

    Django-Rest-Auth — 134

    User Registration — 140

    Tokens — 145

| Conclusion | 152 |

Chapter 8: Viewsets and Routers — 155
User endpoints	155
Viewsets	161
Routers	163
Conclusion	168

Chapter 9: Schemas and Documentation — 171
Schemas	172
Documentation	174
Django REST Swagger	180
Swagger Log In and Log Out	184
Conclusion	185

Conclusion — 187
| Next Steps | 187 |
| Giving Thanks | 188 |

Acknowledgements — 189

Introduction

The internet is powered by RESTful APIs. Behind the scenes even the simplest online task involves multiple computers interacting with one another.

An API (*Application Programming Interface*) is a formal way to describe two computers communicating directly with one another. And while there are multiple ways to build an API, web APIs–which allow for the transfer of data over the world wide web–are overwhelmingly structured in a RESTful (*REpresentational State Transfer*) pattern.

In this book you will learn how to build multiple RESTful web APIs of increasing complexity from scratch using Django and Django REST Framework.

The combination of Django[1] and Django REST Framework[2] is one of the most popular and customizable ways to build web APIs, used by many of the largest tech companies in the world including Instagram, Mozilla, Pinterest, and Bitbucket. It is also uniquely well-suited to beginners because Django's "batteries-included" approach masks much of the underlying complexity and security risks involved in creating any web API.

Prerequisites

If you're brand new to web development with Django, I recommend first reading my previous book Django for Beginners[3]. The first several chapters are available for free online and cover proper set up, a *Hello World* app, *Pages* app, and a *Message Board* website. The full-length version goes deeper and covers a *Blog* website with forms and

---

[1] https://www.djangoproject.com/
[2] http://www.django-rest-framework.org/
[3] https://djangoforbeginners.com/

user accounts as well as a production-ready *Newspaper* site that features a custom user model, complete user authentication flow, emails, permissions, and more.

This background in traditional Django is important since Django REST Framework deliberately mimics many Django conventions.

It is also recommended that readers have a basic knowledge of Python itself. Truly mastering Python takes years, but with just a little bit of knowledge you can dive right in and start building things.

Why APIs

Django was first released in 2005 and at the time most websites consisted of one large monolithic codebase. The "back-end" consisted of database models, URLs, and views which interacted with the "front-end" templates of HTML, CSS, and JavaScript that controlled the presentational layout of each web page.

However in recent years an "API-first" approach has emerged as arguably the dominant paradigm in web development. This approach involves formally separating the back-end from the front-end. It means Django becomes a powerful database and API instead of just a website framework.

Today Django is arguably used more often as *just* a back-end API rather than a full monolithic website solution at large companies!

An obvious question at this point is, "Why bother?" Traditional Django works quite well on its own and transforming a Django site into a web API *seems* like a lot of extra work. Plus, as a developer, you then have to write a dedicated front-end in *another* programming language.

This approach of dividing services into different components, by the way, is broadly known as Service-oriented architecture[4].

---

[4]https://en.wikipedia.org/wiki/Service-oriented_architecture

It turns out however that there are multiple advantages to separating the front-end from the back-end. First, it is arguably much more "future-proof" because a back-end API can be consumed by *any* JavaScript front-end. Given the rapid rate of change in front-end libraries–React[5] was only released in 2013 and Vue[6] in 2014!–this is highly valuable. When the current front-end frameworks are eventually replaced by even newer ones in the years to come, the back-end API can remain the same. No major rewrite is required.

Second, an API can support multiple front-ends written in different languages and frameworks. Consider that JavaScript is used for web front-ends, while Android apps require the Java programming language, and iOS apps need the Swift programming language. With a traditional monolithic approach, a Django website cannot support these various front-ends. But with an internal API, all three can communicate with the same underlying database back-end!

Third, an API-first approach can be used both internally and externally. When I worked at Quizlet[7] back in 2010 we did not have the resources to develop our own iOS or Android apps. But we *did* have an external API available that more than 30 developers used to create their own flashcard apps powered by the Quizlet database. Several of these apps were downloaded over a million times, enriching the developers and increasing the reach of Quizlet at the same time. Quizlet is now a top 20 website in the U.S. during the school year.

The major downside to an API-first approach is that it requires more configuration than a traditional Django application. However as we will see in this book, the fantastic Django REST Framework library removes much of this complexity.

---

[5]https://reactjs.org/
[6]https://vuejs.org/
[7]https://quizlet.com/

Django REST Framework

There are hundreds and hundreds of third-party apps available that add further functionality to Django. (You can see a complete, searchable list over at Django Packages[8].) However Django REST Framework is arguably **the** killer app for Django. It is mature, full of features, customizable, testable, and extremely well-documented. It also purposefully mimics many of Django's traditional conventions, which makes learning it much faster. And it is written in the Python programming language, a wonderful, popular, and accessible language.

If you already know Django, then learning Django REST Framework is a logical next step. With a minimal amount of code, it can transform any existing Django application into a web API.

Why this book

I wrote this book because there is a distinct lack of good resources available for developers new to Django REST Framework. The assumption seems to be that everyone already knows all about APIs, HTTP, REST, and the like. My own journey in learning how to build web APIs was frustrating...and I already knew Django well enough to write a book on it!

This book is the guide I wish existed when starting out with Django REST Framework.

Chapter 1 begins with a brief introduction to web APIs and the HTTP protocol. In **Chapter 2** we review the differences between traditional Django and Django REST Framework by building out a *Library* book website and then adding an API to it. Then in **Chapters 3-4** we build a *Todo* API and connect it to a React front-end. The same

---
[8]https://djangopackages.org/

process can be used to connect any dedicated front-end–web, iOS, Android, desktop, or other–to a web API back-end.

In **Chapters 5-9** we build out a production-ready *Blog* API which includes full CRUD functionality. We also cover in-depth permissions, user authentication, viewsets, routers, documentation, and more.

Complete source code for all chapters can be found online on Github[9].

Conclusion

Django and Django REST Framework is a powerful and accessible way to build web APIs. By the end of this book you will be able to build your own web APIs from scratch properly using modern best practices. And you'll be able to extend any existing Django website into a web API with a minimal amount of code.

Let's begin!

---
[9]https://github.com/wsvincent/restapiswithdjango

Chapter 1: Web APIs

Before we start building our own web APIs it's important to review how the web really works, since after all a "web API" literally sits on top of the existing architecture of the world wide web and relies on a host of technologies including HTTP, IP/TCP, and more.

In this chapter we will review the basic terminology of web APIs: endpoints, resources, HTTP verbs, HTTP status codes, and REST. Even if you already feel comfortable with these terms, I encourage you to read the chapter in full.

World Wide Web

The Internet is a system of interconnected computer networks that has existed since at least the 1960s[10]. However the internet's early usage was restricted to a small number of isolated networks, largely government, military, or scientific in nature, that exchanged information electronically. By the 1980s many research institutes and universities were also using the internet to share data. In Europe the biggest internet node was located at CERN (European Organization for Nuclear Research) in Geneva, Switzerland, which operates the largest particle physics laboratory in the world. These experiments generate enormous quantities of data that need to be shared remotely with scientists all around the world.

Compared with today though, overall internet usage up to the 1980s was miniscule. Most people did not have access to it or even understood why it mattered. A small

---
[10]https://en.wikipedia.org/wiki/Internet

number of internet nodes powered all the traffic and the computers using it were primarily within the same, small networks.

This all changed in 1989 when a research scientist at CERN, Tim Berners-Lee, invented HTTP and ushered in the modern World Wide Web. His great insight was that the existing hypertext[11] system, where text displayed on a computer screen contained links (hyperlinks) to other documents, could be moved onto the internet.

His invention, Hypertext Transfer Protocol (HTTP)[12], was the first standard, universal way to share documents over the internet. It ushered in the concept of web pages: discrete documents with a URL, links, and resources such as images, audio, or video.

Today when most people think of "the internet" they think of the World Wide Web, which is now the primary way that billions of people and computers communicate online.

URLs

A URL (Uniform Resource Locator) is the address of a resource on the internet. For example, the Google homepage lives at `https://www.google.com`.

When you want to go to the Google homepage, you type the full URL address into a web browser. Your browser then sends a request out over the internet and is magically connected (we'll cover what actually happens shortly) to a server that responds with the data needed to render the Google homepage in your browser.

This **request** and **response** pattern is the basis of all web communication. A **client** (typically a web browser but also a native app or really any internet-connected device) requests information and a **server**, somewhere, responds with a response.

---

[11]https://en.wikipedia.org/wiki/Hypertext
[12]https://en.wikipedia.org/wiki/Hypertext_Transfer_Protocol

Since web communication occurs via HTTP these are known more formally as HTTP requests and HTTP responses.

Within a given URL are also several discrete components. For example, consider again `https://www.google.com`. The first part, `https`, refers to the **scheme** used. It tells the web browser *how* to access resources at the location. For a website this is typically `http` or `https`, but it could also be `ftp` for files, `smtp` for email, and so on. The next section, `www.google.com`, is the **hostname** or the actual name of the site. Every URL contains a scheme and a host.

Many webpages also contain an optional **path**, too. If you go to the homepage for Python at `https://www.python.org` and click on the link for the "About" page you'll be redirected to `https://www.python.org/about/`. The `/about/` piece is the path.

In summary, every URL like `https://python.org/about/` has three potential parts:

- a scheme - `https`
- a hostname - `www.python.org`
- and an (optional) path - `/about/`

Internet Protocol Suite

Once we know the actual URL of a resource, a whole collection of other technologies must work properly (together) to connect the client with the server and load an actual webpage. This is broadly referred to as the internet procotol suite[13] and there are entire books written on just this topic. For our purposes, however, we can stick to the broad basics.

When a user types `https://www.google.com` into their web browser and hits enter, several things happen. First the browser needs to find the desired server, somewhere,

---
[13] https://en.wikipedia.org/wiki/Internet_protocol_suite

on the vast internet. It uses a *domain name service* (DNS) to translate the domain name "google.com" into an IP address[14], which is a unique sequence of numbers representing every connected device on the internet. Domain names are used because it is easier for humans to remember a domain name like "google.com" than an IP address like "2001:0db8:0000:0042:0000:8a2e:0370:7334".

After the browser has the IP address for a given domain, it needs a way to set up a consistent connection with the desired server. This happens via the *Transmission Control Protocol* (TCP) which provides reliable, ordered, and error-checked delivery of bytes between two application.

To establish a TCP connection between two computers, a three-way "handshake" occurs between the client and server:

1. The client sends a `SYN` asking to establish a connection
2. The server responds with a `SYN-ACK` acknowledging the request and passing a connection parameter
3. The client sends an `ACK` back to the server confirming the connection

Once the TCP connection is established, the two computers can start communicating via HTTP.

HTTP Verbs

Every webpage contains both an address (the URL) as well as a list of approved actions known as HTTP verbs. So far we've mainly talked about getting a web page, but it's also possible to create, edit, and delete content.

Consider the Facebook website. After logging in, you can read your timeline, create a new post, or edit/delete an existing one. These four actions Create-Read-Update-

---
[14]https://en.wikipedia.org/wiki/IP_address

Delete are known colloquially as CRUD functionality and represent the overwhelming majority of actions taken online.

The HTTP protocol contains a number of request methods[15] that can be used while requesting information from a server. The four most common map to CRUD functionality. They are POST, GET, PUT, and DELETE.

Diagram

```
CRUD                              HTTP Verbs
----                              ----------
Create   <-------------------->   POST
Read     <-------------------->   GET
Update   <-------------------->   PUT
Delete   <-------------------->   DELETE
```

To create content you use POST, to read content GET, to update it PUT, and to delete it you use DELETE.

Endpoints

A website consists of web pages with HTML, CSS, images, JavaScript, and more. But a web API has *endpoints* instead which are URLs with a list of available actions (HTTP verbs) that expose data (typically in JSON[16], which is the most common data format these days and the default for Django REST Framework).

For example, we could create the following API endpoints for a new website called `mysite`.

---

[15]https://en.wikipedia.org/wiki/Hypertext_Transfer_Protocol#Request_method
[16]https://json.org/

Diagram

```
https://www.mysite.com/api/users      # GET returns a collection of all users
https://www.mysite.com/api/users/<id> # GET returns a single user
```

In the first endpoint, /api/users, an available GET request returns a list of all available users. This type of endpoint which returns multiple data resources is known as a **collection**.

The second endpoint /api/users/<id> represents a single user. A GET request returns information about just that one user.

If we added POST to the first endpoint we could create a new user, while adding DELETE to the second endpoint would allow us to delete a single user.

We will become much more familiar with API endpoints over the course of this book but ultimately creating an API involves making a series of endpoints: URLs with associated HTTP verbs.

A webpage consists of HTML, CSS, images, and more. But an endpoint is *just* a way to access data via the available HTTP verbs.

HTTP

We've already talked a lot about HTTP in this chapter, but here we will describe what it actually is and how it works.

HTTP is a *request-response* protocol between two computers that have an existing TCP connection. The computer making the requests is known as the *client* while the computer responding is known as the *server*. Typically a client is a web browser but it could also be an iOS app or really any internet-connected device. A server is a fancy name for any computer optimized to work over the internet. All we really need to transform a basic laptop into a server is some special software and a persistent internet connection.

Every HTTP message consists of a request/status line, headers, and optional body data. For example, here is a sample HTTP message that a browser might send to request the Google homepage located at `http://www.google.com`.

Diagram

```
GET / HTTP/1.1
Host: google.com
Accept_Language: en-US
```

The top line is known as the *request line* and it specifies the HTTP method to use (GET), the path (/), and the specific version of HTTP to use (HTTP/1.1).

The two subsequent lines are HTTP headers: Host is the domain name and Accept_Language is the language to use, in this case American English. There are many HTTP headers[17] available.

HTTP messages also have an optional third section, known as the body. However we only see a body message with HTTP responses containing data.

For simplicity, let's assume that the Google homepage only contained the HTML "Hello, World!" This is what the HTTP response message from a Google server might look like.

---

[17]https://en.wikipedia.org/wiki/List_of_HTTP_header_fields

Diagram

```
HTTP/1.1 200 OK

Date: Wed, 02 Sep 2018 23:26:07 GMT

Server: Apache/2.2.8 (Ubuntu) mod_ssl/2.2.8 OpenSSL/0.9.8g

Last-Modified: Wed, 03 May 2018 12:02:55 GMT

ETag: "45b6-834-49130cc1182c0"

Accept-Ranges: bytes

Content-Length: 13

Connection: close

Content-Type: text/html


Hello, world!
```

The top line is the *response line* and it specifies that we are using `HTTP/1.1`. The status code `200 OK` indicates the request by the client was successful (more on status codes shortly).

The next eight lines are HTTP headers. And finally *after a line break* there is our actual body content of "Hello, world!".

Every HTTP message, whether a request or response, therefore has the following format:

Diagram

```
Response/request line

Headers...


(optional) Body
```

Most web pages contain multiple resources that require multiple HTTP request/response cycles. If a webpage had HTML, one CSS file, and an image, three separate trips back-and-forth between the client and server would be required before the complete web page could be rendered in the browser.

Status Codes

Once your web browser has executed an HTTP Request on a URL there is no guarantee things will actually work! Thus there is a quite lengthy list of HTTP Status Codes[18] available to accompany each HTTP response.

You can tell the general *type* of status code based on the following system:

- 2xx Success - the action requested by the client was received, understood, and accepted
- 3xx Redirection - the requested URL has moved
- 4xx Client Error - there was an error, typically a bad URL request by the client
- 5xx Server Error - the server failed to resolve a request

There is no need to memorize all the available status codes. With practice you will become familiar with the most common ones such as 200 (OK), 201 (Created), 301 (Moved Permanently), 404 (Not Found), and 500 (Server Error).

[18]https://en.wikipedia.org/wiki/List_of_HTTP_status_codes

The important thing to remember is that, generally speaking, there are only four potential outcomes to any given HTTP request: it worked (2xx), it was redirected somehow (3xx), the client made an error (4xx), or the server made an error (5xx).

These status codes are automatically placed in the request/response line at the top of every HTTP message.

Statelessness

A final important point to make about HTTP is that it is a **stateless** protocol. This means each request/response pair is completely independent of the previous one. There is no stored memory of past interactions, which is known as state[19] in computer science.

Statelessness brings a lot of benefits to HTTP. Since all electronic communication systems have signal loss over time, if we *did not* have a stateless protocol, things would constantly break if one request/response cycle didn't go through. As a result HTTP is known as a very resilient distributed protocol.

The downside however is that managing state is really, really important in web applications. State is how a website remembers that you've logged in and how an e-commerce site manages your shopping cart. It's fundamental to how we use modern websites, yet it's not supported on HTTP itself.

Historically state was maintained on the server but it has moved more and more to the client, the web browser, in modern front-end frameworks like React, Angular, and Vue. We'll learn more about state when we cover user authentication but remember that HTTP is stateless. This makes it very good for reliably sending information between two computers, but bad at remembering anything outside of each individual request/response pair.

---

[19]https://en.wikipedia.org/wiki/State_(computer_science)

REST

REpresentational State Transfer (REST)[20] is an architecture first proposed in 2000 by Roy Fielding in his dissertation thesis. It is an approach to building APIs on top of the web, which means on top of the HTTP protocol.

Entire books have been written on what makes an API actually RESTful or not. But there are three main traits that we will focus on here for our purposes. Every RESTful API:

- is stateless, like HTTP
- supports common HTTP verbs (GET, POST, PUT, DELETE, etc.)
- returns data in either the JSON or XML format

Any RESTful API must, at a minimum, have these three principles. The standard is important because it provides a consistent way to both design and consume web APIs.

Conclusion

While there is **a lot** of technology underlying the modern world wide web, we as developers don't have to implement it all from scratch. The beautiful combination of Django and Django REST Framework handles, properly, most of the complexity involved with web APIs. However it is important to have at least a broad understanding of how all the pieces fit together.

Ultimately a web API is a collection of endpoints that expose certain parts of an underlying database. As developers we control the URLs for each endpoint, what underlying data is available, and what actions are possible via HTTP verbs. By using

---

[20]https://en.wikipedia.org/wiki/Representational_state_transfer

HTTP headers we can set various levels of authentication and permission too as we will see later in the book.

Chapter 2: Library Website and API

Django REST Framework works alongside the Django web framework to create web APIs. We cannot build a web API with *only* Django Rest Framework; it always must be added to a project *after* Django itself has been installed and configured.

In this chapter we will review the similarities and differences between traditional Django and Django REST Framework. The most important takeaway is that Django creates websites containing webpages, while Django REST Framework creates web APIs which are a collection of URL endpoints containing available HTTP verbs that return JSON.

To illustrate these concepts, we will build out a basic *Library* website with traditional Django and then extend it into a web API with Django REST Framework.

Make sure you already have Python 3 and Pipenv[21] installed on your computer. Complete instructions can be found here[22] if you need help.

Traditional Django

First we need a dedicated directory on our computer to store the code. This can live anywhere but for convenience, if you are on a Mac, we can place it in the Desktop folder. The location really does not matter; it just needs to be easily accessible.

---

[21]https://docs.pipenv.org/
[22]https://djangoforbeginners.com/initial-setup/

Command Line

```
$ cd ~/Desktop
$ mkdir code && cd code
$ mkdir library && cd library
```

Now we are within the `code` folder which will be the location for all the code in this book. The next step is to create a dedicated directory for our `library` site, install Django via Pipenv, and then enter the virtual environment using the `shell` command. You should always use a dedicated virtual environment for every new Python project.

Command Line

```
$ pipenv install django==2.1
$ pipenv shell
(library) $
```

Pipenv creates a `Pipfile` and a `Pipfile.lock` within our current directory. The `(library)` in parentheses before the command line shows that our virtual environment is active. The actual name will look something like `(library-XXXX)` where the XXXX is a random string of characters, but it is shortened to `(library)` here for brevity.

A traditional Django website consists of a single *project* and one (or more) *apps* representing discrete functionality. Let's create a new project with the `startproject` command. Don't forget to include the period . at the end which installs the code in our current directory. If you do not include the period, Django will create an additional directory by default.

Command Line

```
(library) $ django-admin startproject library_project .
```

Django automatically generates a new project for us which we can see with the `tree` command. (Note: If tree doesn't work for you on a Mac, install it with Homebrew[23]: `brew install tree`.)

Command Line

```
(library) $ tree
.
├── Pipfile
├── Pipfile.lock
├── library_project
│   ├── __init__.py
│   ├── settings.py
│   ├── urls.py
│   └── wsgi.py
└── manage.py
```

The files have the following roles:

- `__init__.py` is a Python way to treat a directory as a package; it is empty
- `settings.py` contains all the configuration for our project
- `urls.py` controls the top-level URL routes
- `wsgi.py` stands for *web server gateway interface* and helps Django serve the eventual web pages
- `manage.py` executes various Django commands such as running the local web server or creating a new app.

---
[23]https://brew.sh/

Run `migrate` to sync the database with Django's default settings and start up the local Django web server.

Command Line

```
(library) $ python manage.py migrate
(library) $ python manage.py runserver
```

Open a web browser to http://127.0.0.1:8000/[24] to confirm our project is successfully installed.

[24] http://127.0.0.1:8000/

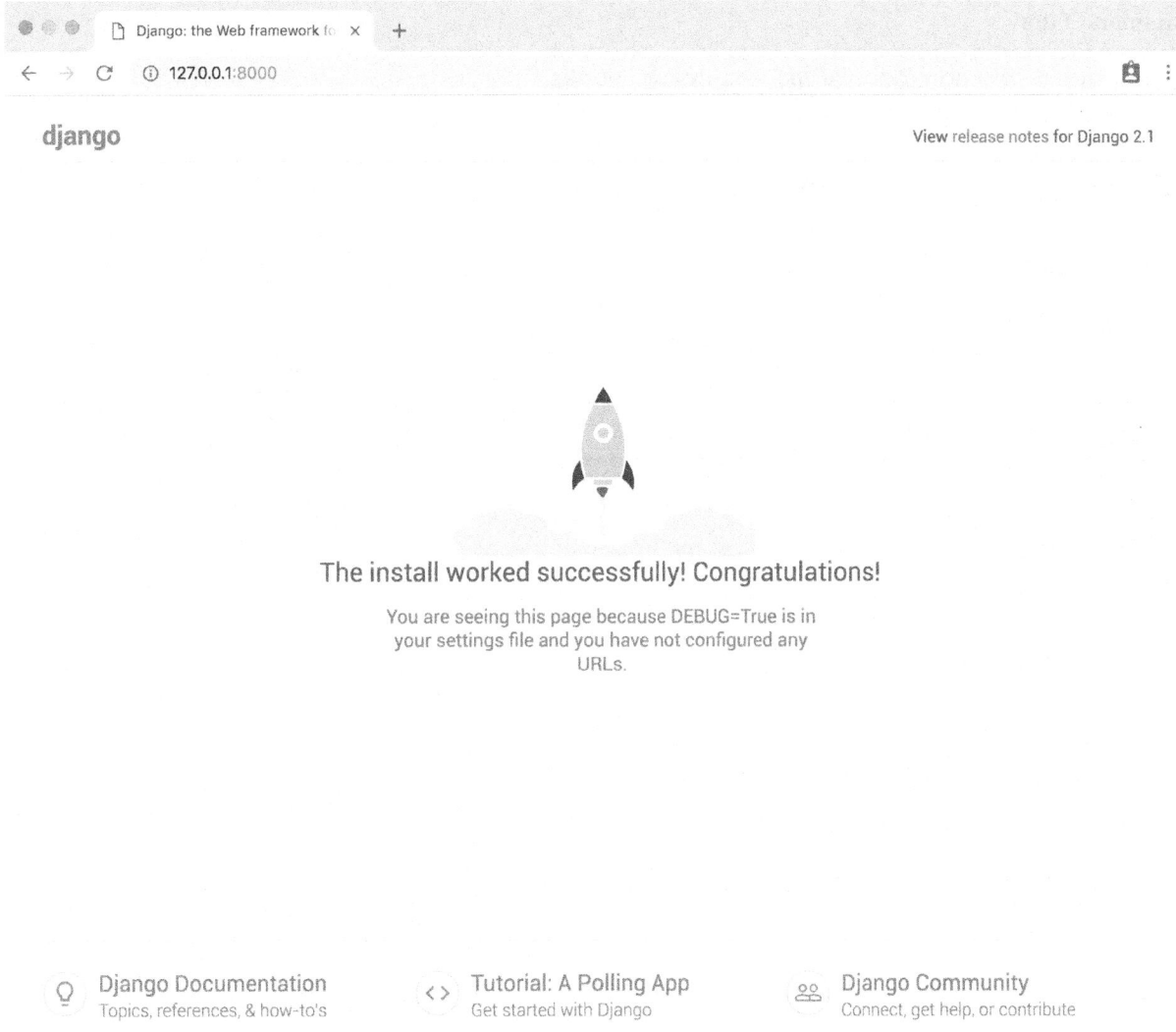

Django welcome page

First app

The typical next step is to start adding *apps*, which represent discrete areas of functionality. A single Django project can support multiple apps.

Stop the local server by typing `Control+c` and then create a `books` app.

Command Line

```
(library) $ python manage.py startapp books
```

Now let's see what files Django has generated.

Command Line

```
(library) $ tree
.
├── Pipfile
├── Pipfile.lock
├── books
│   ├── __init__.py
│   ├── admin.py
│   ├── apps.py
│   ├── migrations
│   │   └── __init__.py
│   ├── models.py
│   ├── tests.py
│   └── views.py
├── library_project
│   ├── __init__.py
│   ├── settings.py
│   ├── urls.py
│   └── wsgi.py
└── manage.py
```

Each app has a `__init__.py` file identifying it as a Python package. There are 6 new files created:

- `admin.py` is a configuration file for the built-in Django Admin app

- `apps.py` is a configuration file for the app itself
- the `migrations/` directory stores migrations files for database changes
- `models.py` is where we define our database models
- `tests.py` is for our app-specific tests
- `views.py` is where we handle the request/response logic for our web app

Typically developers will also create an `urls.py` file within each app too for routing.

Let's build out the files so that our *Library* project lists out all books on the homepage. Open the text editor of your choice to the `settings.py` file. The first step is to add the new app to our `INSTALLED_APPS` configuration. We always add new apps at the bottom since Django will read them in order and we want the built-in core Django apps like `admin` and `auth` to already be loaded before it loads ours.

Code

```python
# library_project/settings.py
INSTALLED_APPS = [
    'django.contrib.admin',
    'django.contrib.auth',
    'django.contrib.contenttypes',
    'django.contrib.sessions',
    'django.contrib.messages',
    'django.contrib.staticfiles',

    # Local
    'books.apps.BooksConfig', # new
]
```

Then run `migrate` to sync our database with the changes.

Command Line

```
(library) $ python manage.py migrate
```

Each web page in traditional Django requires several files: a view, url, and template. But first we need a database model so let's start there.

Models

In your text editor, open up the file `books/models.py` and update it as follows:

Code

```python
# books/models.py
from django.db import models


class Book(models.Model):
    title = models.CharField(max_length=250)
    subtitle = models.CharField(max_length=250)
    author = models.CharField(max_length=100)
    isbn = models.CharField(max_length=13)

    def __str__(self):
        return self.title
```

This is a basic Django model where we import `models` from Django on the top line and then create a `Book` class that extends it. There are four fields: title, subtitle, author, and isbn. We also include a `__str__` method so that the title of a book will display in the admin later on.

Note that an ISBN[25] is a unique, 13-character identifier assigned to every published book.

Since we created a new database model we need to create a migration file to go along with it. Specifying the app name is optional but recommended here. We *could* just type `python manage.py makemigrations` but if there were multiple apps with database changes, both would be added to the migrations file which makes debugging in the future more of a challenge. Keep your migrations files as specific as possible.

Then run `migrate` to update our database.

Command Line

```
(library) $ python manage.py makemigrations books
(library) $ python manage.py migrate
```

So far so good. If any of this feels new to you, I suggest you pause and review Django for Beginners[26] for a more-detailed explanation of traditional Django.

Admin

We can start entering data into our new model via the built-in Django app. But we must do two things first: create a superuser account and update `admin.py` so the `books` app is displayed.

Start with the superuser account. On the command line run the following command:

---

[25]https://www.isbn-international.org/content/what-isbn
[26]https://djangoforbeginners.com/

Command Line

```
(library) $ python manage.py createsuperuser
```

Follow the prompts to enter a username, email, and password. Note that for security reasons, text will not appear on the screen while entering your password.

Now update our `book` app's `admin.py` file.

Code

```python
# books/admin.py
from django.contrib import admin
from .models import Book

admin.site.register(Book)
```

That's all we need! Start up the local server again.

Command Line

```
(library) $ python manage.py runserver
```

Navigate to http://127.0.0.1:8000/admin[27] and log in.

---
[27]http://127.0.0.1:8000/admin

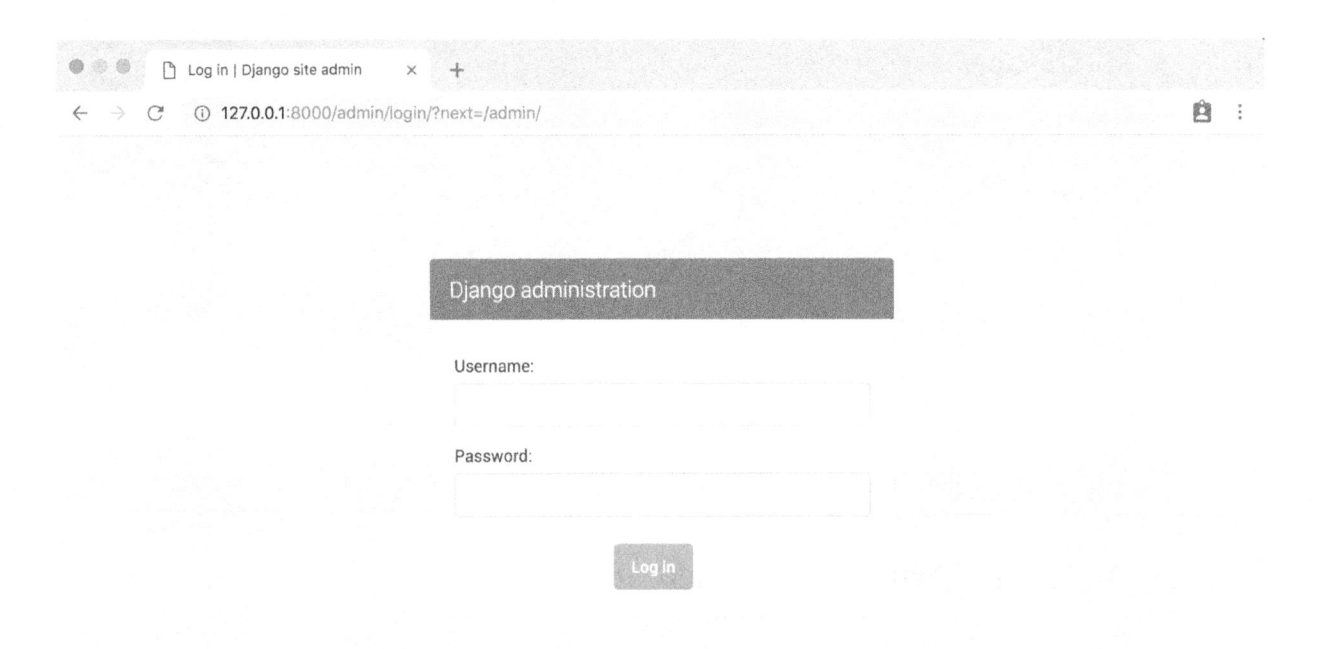

Admin login

You will be redirected to the admin homepage.

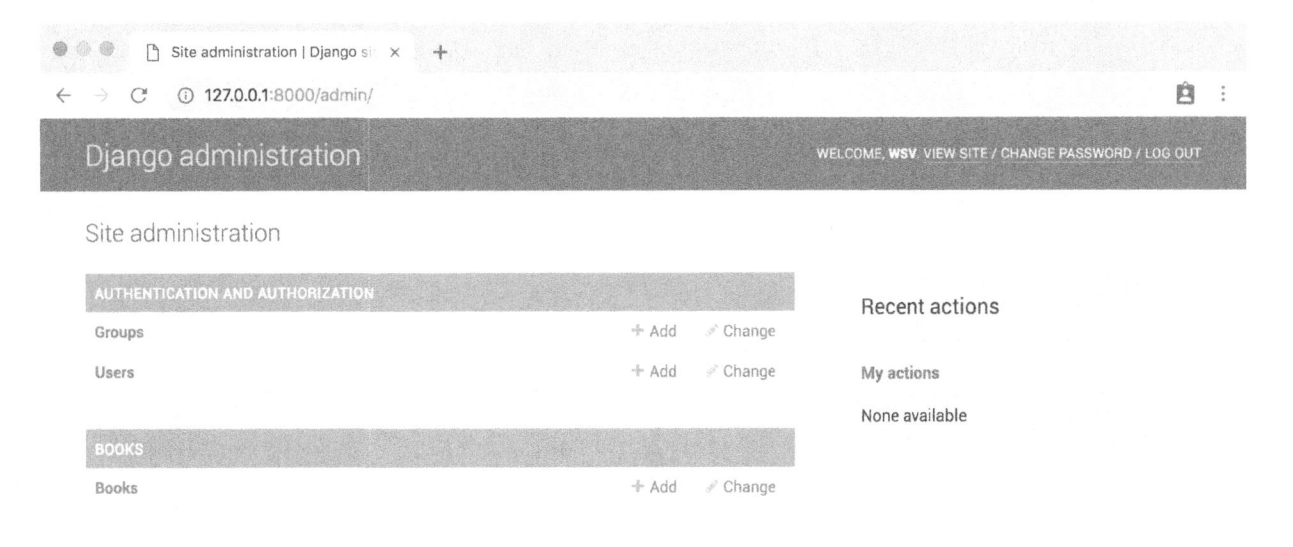

Admin homepage

Click on the link for Books.

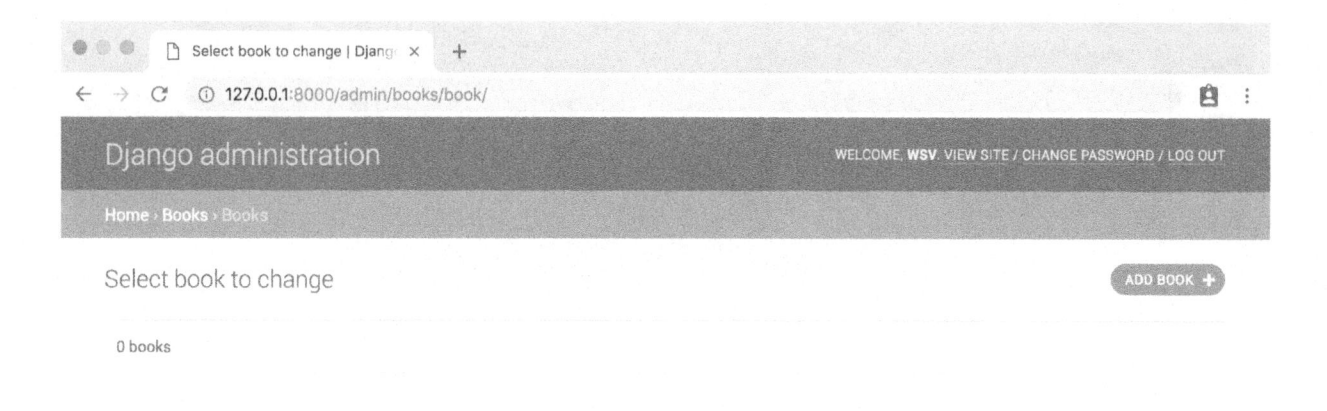

Admin books page

Then the "Add Book +" button in the upper righthand corner.

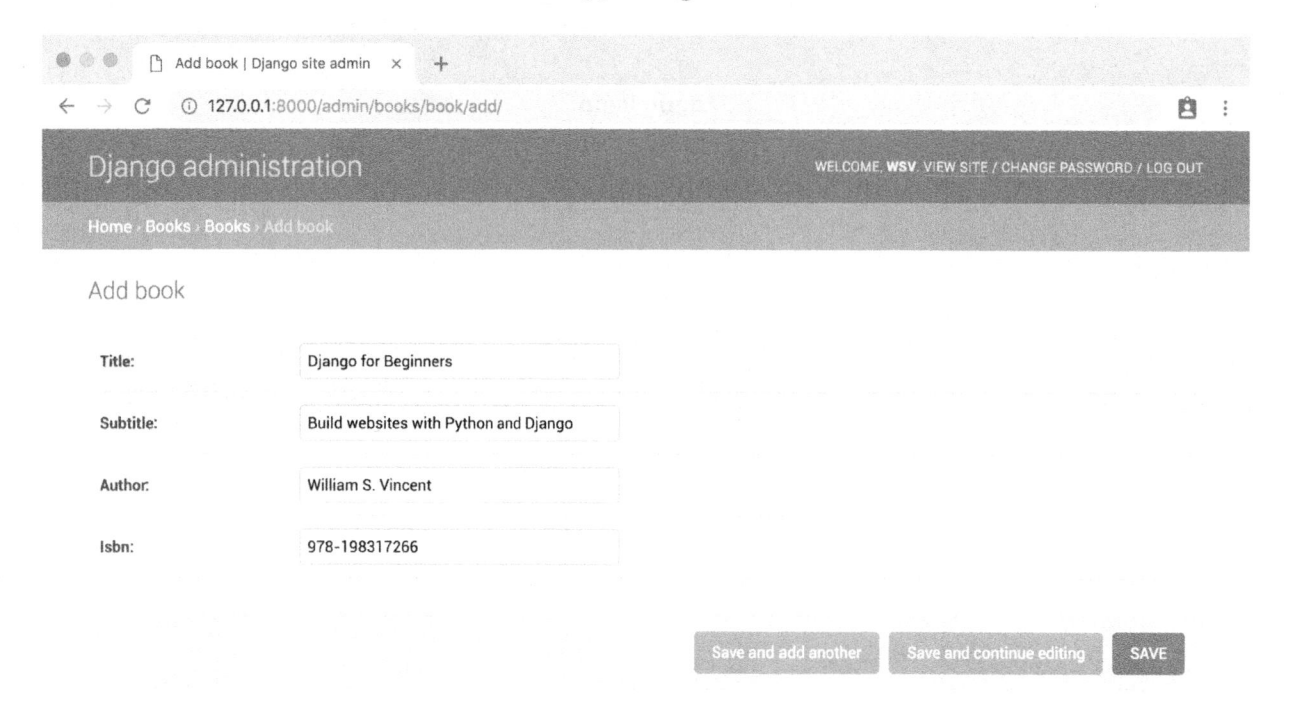

Admin add book

I've entered in the details for my Django for Beginners book. You can enter whatever text you want here. It's purely for demonstration purposes. After clicking the "Save" button we are redirected to the "Books" page that lists all current entries.

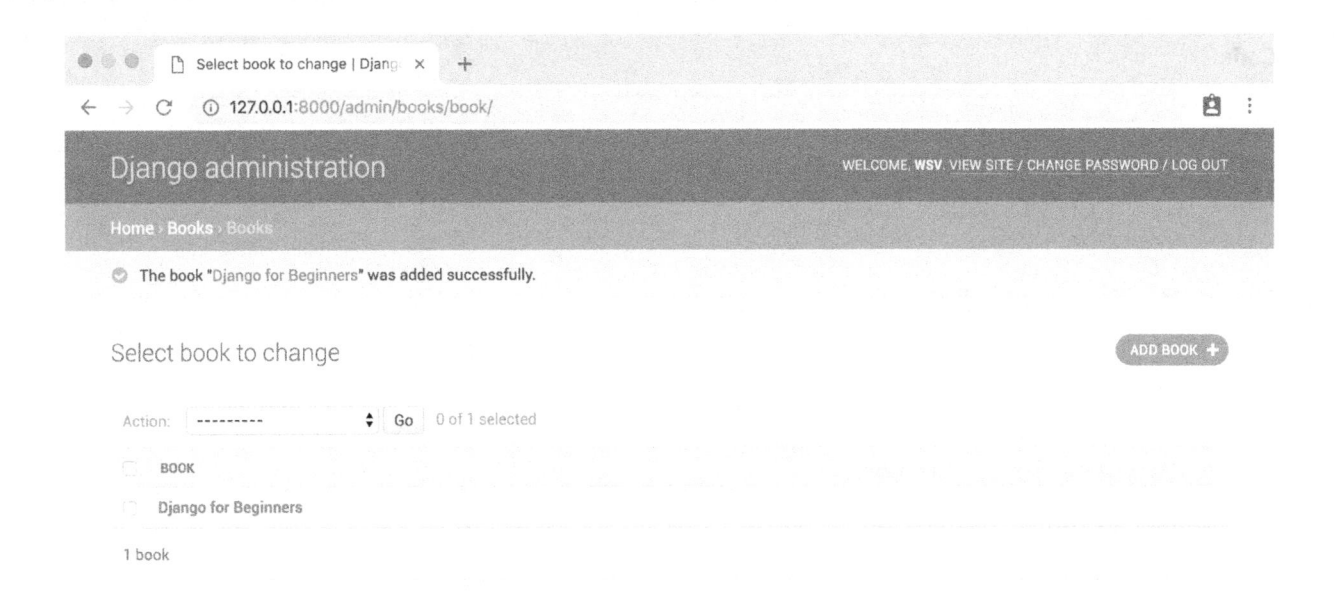

Admin books list

Our traditional Django project has data now but we need a way to expose it as a web page. That means creating views, URLs, and template files. Let's do that now.

Views

The `views.py` file controls *how* the database model content is displayed. Since we want to list all books we can use the built-in generic class ListView[28].

Update the `books/views.py` file.

---

[28]https://docs.djangoproject.com/en/2.1/ref/class-based-views/generic-display/#django.views.generic.list.ListView

Code

```
# books/views.py
from django.views.generic import ListView

from .models import Book


class BookListView(ListView):
    model = Book
    template_name = 'book_list.html'
```

On the top lines we've imported `ListView` and our `Book` model. Then we create a `BookListView` class that specifies the model to use and the template (not created yet).

Two more steps before we have a working web page: make our template and configure our URLs. Let's start with the URLs.

URLs

We need to set up both the project-level `urls.py` file and then one within the `books` app. When a user visits our site they will first interact with the `library_project/urls.py` file so let's configure that first.

Code

```
# library_project/urls.py
from django.contrib import admin
from django.urls import path, include # new

urlpatterns = [
    path('admin/', admin.site.urls),
    path('', include('books.urls')), # new
]
```

The top two lines import the built-in `admin` app, `path` for our routes, and `include` which will be used with our `books` app. If a user goes to /admin/ they will be redirected to the `admin` app. We use the empty string `''` for the `books` app route which means a user on the homepage will be redirected directly to the `books` app.

Now we can configure our `books/urls.py` file. But, oops! Django for some reason does not include a `urls.py` file by default in apps so we need to create it ourself.

Command Line

```
(library) $ touch books/urls.py
```

Now within a text editor update the new file.

Code

```
# books/urls.py
from django.urls import path

from .views import BookListView

urlpatterns = [
    path('', BookListView.as_view(), name='home'),
]
```

We import our views file, configure `BookListView` at the empty string `''`, and add a named URL[29] `home` as a best practice.

The way Django works, now when a user goes to the homepage of our website they will first hit the `library_project/urls.py` file, then be redirected to `books/urls.py` which specifies using the `BookListView`. In this view file, the `Book` model is used along with `ListView` to list out all books.

The final step is to create our template file that controls the layout on the actual web page. We have already specified its name as `book_list.html` in our view. There are two options for its location: by default the Django template loader will look for templates within our `books` app in the following location: `books/templates/books/book_list.html`. We could also create a separate, project-level `templates` directory instead and update our `settings.py` file to point there.

Which one you ultimately use in your own projects is a personal preference. We will use the default structure here. If you are curious about the second approach, check out the book Django For Beginners[30].

---

[29]https://docs.djangoproject.com/en/2.1/topics/http/urls/#naming-url-patterns
[30]https://wsvincent.com/django-for-beginners/

Start by making a new `templates` folder within the `books` app, then within it a `books` folder, and finally a `book_list.html` file.

Command Line

```
(library) $ mkdir books/templates
(library) $ mkdir books/templates/books
(library) $ touch books/templates/books/book_list.html
```

Now update the template file.

HTML

```html
<!-- books/templates/books/book_list.html -->
<h1>All books</h1>
{% for book in object_list %}
  <ul>
    <li>Title: {{ book.title }}</li>
    <li>Subtitle: {{ book.subtitle }}</li>
    <li>Author: {{ book.author }}</li>
    <li>ISBN: {{ book.isbn }}</li>
  </ul>
{% endfor %}
```

Django ships with a template language[31] that allows for basic logic. Here we use the for[32] tag to loop over all available books. Template tags must be included within opening/closing brackets and parentheses. So the format is always `{% for ... %}` and then we must close our loop later with `{% endfor %}`.

What we are looping over is the object containing all available books in our model courtesy of `ListView`. The name of this object is `object_list`. Therefore to loop over

---

[31] https://docs.djangoproject.com/en/2.1/ref/templates/language/
[32] https://docs.djangoproject.com/en/2.1/ref/templates/builtins/#std:templatetag-for

each book we write `{% for book in object_list %}`. And then display each field from our model.

Webpage

Now we can start up the local Django server and see our web page.

Command Line
```
(library) $ python manage.py runserver
```

Navigate to the homepage which is at http://127.0.0.1:8000/[33].

Book web page

If we add additional books in the admin, they will each appear here, too.

This was a very quick run-through of a traditional Django website. Now let's add an API to it!

Django REST Framework

Django REST Framework is added just like any other third-party app. Make sure to quit the local server `Control+c` if it is still running. Then on the command line type the below.

---
[33] http://127.0.0.1:8000/

Command Line

```
(library) $ pipenv install djangorestframework==3.8.2
```

Add `rest_framework` to the `INSTALLED_APPS` config in our `settings.py` file. I like to make a distinction between third-party apps and local apps as follows since the number of apps grows quickly in most projects.

Code

```
# library_project/settings.py
INSTALLED_APPS = [
    'django.contrib.admin',
    'django.contrib.auth',
    'django.contrib.contenttypes',
    'django.contrib.sessions',
    'django.contrib.messages',
    'django.contrib.staticfiles',

    # 3rd party
    'rest_framework', # new

    # Local
    'books.apps.BooksConfig',
]
```

Ultimately our API will expose a single endpoint that lists out all books in JSON. So we will need a new URL route, a new view, and a new serializer file (more on this shortly).

There are multiple ways we can organize these files however my preferred approach is to create a dedicated `api` app. That way even if we add more apps in the future, each app can contain the models, views, templates, and urls needed for dedicated webpages, but all API-specific files for the entire project will live in a dedicated `api` app.

Let's first create a new `api` app.

Command Line

```
(library) $ python manage.py startapp api
```

Then add it to `INSTALLED_APPS`.

Code

```python
# library_project/settings.py
INSTALLED_APPS = [
    'django.contrib.admin',
    'django.contrib.auth',
    'django.contrib.contenttypes',
    'django.contrib.sessions',
    'django.contrib.messages',
    'django.contrib.staticfiles',

    # 3rd party
    'rest_framework',

    # Local
    'books.apps.BooksConfig',
    'api.apps.ApiConfig', # new
]
```

The `api` app will not have its own database models so there is no need to create a migration file and update the database as we normally would.

URLs

Let's start with our URL configs. Adding an API endpoint is just like configuring a traditional Django app's routes. First at the project-level we need to include the api app and configure its URL route, which will be api/.

Code

```python
# library_project/urls.py
from django.contrib import admin
from django.urls import path, include

urlpatterns = [
    path('admin/', admin.site.urls),
    path('', include('books.urls')),
    path('api/', include('api.urls')), # new
]
```

Then create a urls.py file within the api app.

Command Line

```
(library) $ touch api/urls.py
```

And update it as follows:

Code

```
# api/urls.py
from django.urls import path

from .views import BookAPIView

urlpatterns = [
    path('', BookAPIView.as_view()),
]
```

All set.

Views

Next up is our `views.py` file which relies on Django REST Framework's built-in generic class views. These deliberately mimic traditional Django's generic class-based views in format, but they are **not** the same thing.

To avoid confusion, some developers will call an API views file `apiviews.py` or `api.py`. Personally, when working within a dedicated `api` app I do not find it confusing to just call a Django REST Framework views file `views.py` but opinion varies on this point.

Within our `views.py` file, update it to look like the following:

Code

```python
# api/views.py
from rest_framework import generics

from books.models import Book
from .serializers import BookSerializer


class BookAPIView(generics.ListAPIView):
    queryset = Book.objects.all()
    serializer_class = BookSerializer
```

On the top lines we import Django REST Framework's `generics` class of views, the models from our `books` app, and `serializers` from our `api` app (we will make the serializers next).

Then we create a `BookAPIView` that uses `ListAPIView` to create a read-only endpoint for all book instances. There are many generic views available and we will explore them further in later chapters.

The only two steps required in our view are to specify the `queryset` which is all available books, and then the `serializer_class` which will be `BookSerializer`.

Serializers

A serializer translates data into a format that is easy to consume over the internet, typically JSON, and is displayed at an API endpoint. We will also cover serializers and JSON in more depth in following chapters. For now I want to demonstrate how easy it is to create a serializer with Django REST Framework to convert Django models to JSON.

Make a `serializers.py` file within our `api` app.

Command Line

```
(library) $ touch api/serializers.py
```

Then update it as follows in a text editor.

Code

```python
# api/serializers.py
from rest_framework import serializers

from books.models import Book


class BookSerializer(serializers.ModelSerializer):
    class Meta:
        model = Book
        fields = ('title', 'subtitle', 'author', 'isbn')
```

On the top lines we import Django REST Framework's `serializers` class and the `Book` model from our `books` app. We extend Django REST Framework's `ModelSerializer` into a `BookSerializer` class that specifies our database model `Book` and the database fields we wish to expose: `title`, `subtitle`, `author`, and `isbn`.

That's it! We're done.

cURL

We want to see what our API endpoint looks like. We know it should return JSON at the URL http://127.0.0.1:8000/api/[34]. Let's ensure that our local Django server is

---
[34] http://127.0.0.1:8000/api/

running:

Command Line

```
(library) $ python manage.py runserver
```

Now open a new, second command line console. We will use it to access the API running in the existing command line console.

We can use the popular cURL[35] program to execute HTTP requests via the command line. All we need for a basic GET request it to specify `curl` and the URL we want to call.

Command Line

```
$ curl http://127.0.0.1:8000/api/
[
    {
        "title":"Django for Beginners",
        "subtitle":"Build websites with Python and Django",
        "author":"William S. Vincent",
        "isbn":"978-198317266"
    }
]
```

The data is all there, in JSON format, but it is poorly formatted and hard to make sense of. Fortunately Django REST Framework has a further surprise for us: a powerful visual mode for our API endpoints.

---
[35]https://en.wikipedia.org/wiki/CURL

Browsable API

With the local server still running in the first command line console, navigate to our API endpoint in the web browser at http://127.0.0.1:8000/api/[36].

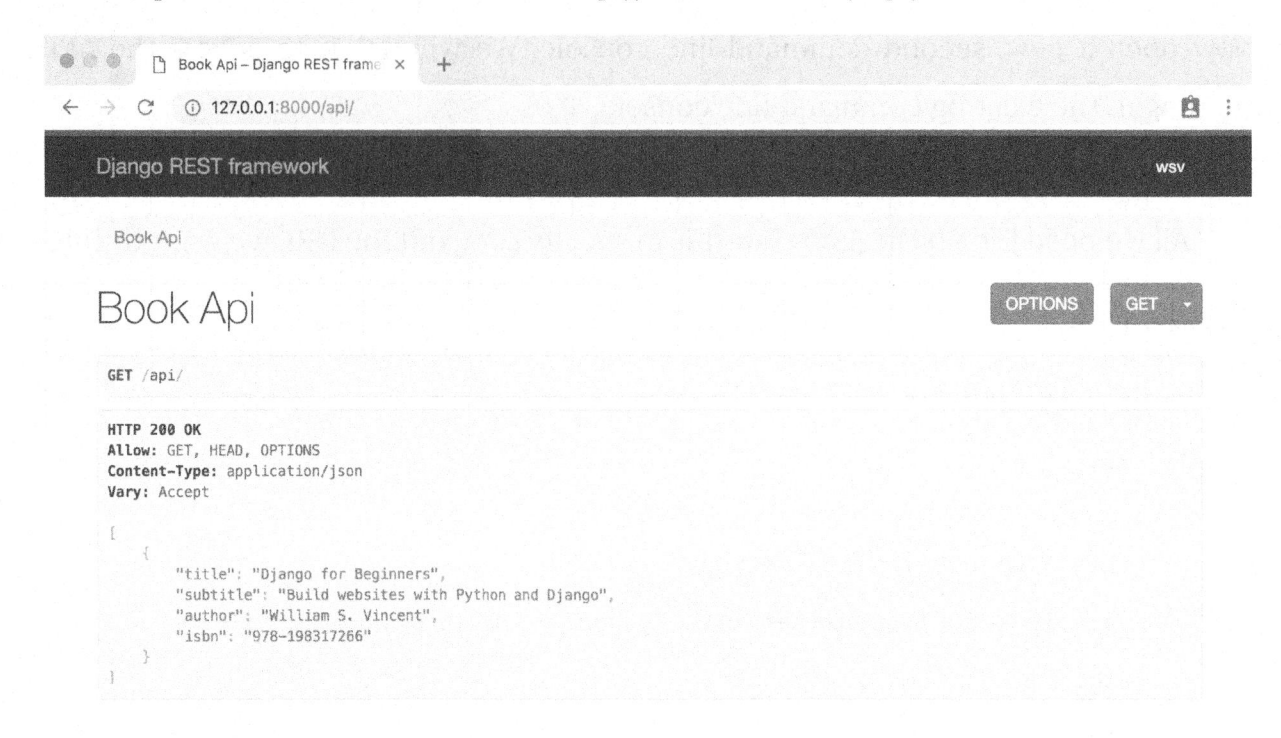

![Book Api browsable API screenshot]

Book API

Wow look at that! Django REST Framework provides this visualization by default. And there is a lot of functionality built into this page that we will explore throughout the book. For now I want you to compare this page with the raw JSON endpoint. Click on the "GET" button and select "json" from the dropdown menu.

---
[36]http://127.0.0.1:8000/api/

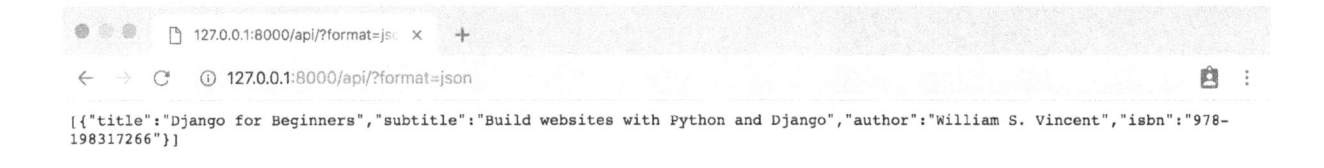

[{"title":"Django for Beginners","subtitle":"Build websites with Python and Django","author":"William S. Vincent","isbn":"978-198317266"}]

Book API JSON

This is what the raw JSON from our API endpoint looks like. I think we can agree the Django REST Framework version is more appealing.

Conclusion

We covered a lot of material in this chapter so don't worry if things feel a little confusing right now. First we created a traditional Django *Library* website. Then we added Django REST Framework and were able to add an API endpoint with a minimal amount of code.

In the next two chapters we will build our own *Todo* API back-end and connect it with a React-powered front-end to demonstrate a complete working example that will help solidify how all this theory fits together in practice!

Chapter 3: Todo API

Over the course of the next two chapters we will build a *Todo* API back-end and then connect it with a React front-end. We have already made our first API and reviewed how HTTP and REST work in the abstract but it's still likely you don't "quite" see how it all fits together yet. By the end of these two chapters you will.

Since we are making a dedicated back-end and front-end we will divide our code into a similar structure. Within our existing `code` directory, we will create a `todo` directory containing our back-end Django Python code and our front-end React JavaScript code.

The eventual layout will look like this.

Diagram

```
todo
|   ├──frontend
|       ├──React...
|   ├──backend
|       ├──Django...
```

This chapter focuses on the back-end and Chapter 4 on the front-end.

Initial Set Up

The first step for any Django API is always to install Django and then later add Django REST Framework on top of it. First create a dedicated `todo` directory within our `code` directory on the Desktop.

Open a new command line console and enter the following commands:

Command Line

```
$ cd ~/Desktop
$ cd code
$ mkdir todo && cd todo
```

Note: Make sure you have deactivated the virtual environment from the previous chapter. You can do this by typing `exit`. Are there no more parentheses in front of your command line? Good. Then you are not in an existing virtual environment.

Within this `todo` folder will be our `backend` and `frontend` directories. Let's create the `backend` folder, install Django, and activate a new virtual environment.

Command Line

```
$ mkdir backend && cd backend
$ pipenv install django==2.1
$ pipenv shell
```

You should see parentheses on your command line confirming the virtual environment is activated. On my computer I see `(backend-NVztdMFH) $`. Your computer will have the same format of `(backend-XXX)` where the `XXX` will be different for each of us. I've shortened the name of the virtual environment to `backend` going forward for brevity.

Now that Django is installed we should start by creating a traditional Django project `todo_project`, adding our first app `todos` within it, and then migrating our initial database.

Command Line

```
(backend) $ django-admin startproject todo_project .
(backend) $ python manage.py startapp todos
(backend) $ python manage.py migrate
```

In Django we always need to add new apps to our INSTALLED_APPS setting so do that now. Open up `todo_project/settings.py` in your text editor. At the bottom of the file add `todos.apps.TodosConfig`.

Code

```
# todo_project/settings.py
INSTALLED_APPS = [
    'django.contrib.admin',
    'django.contrib.auth',
    'django.contrib.contenttypes',
    'django.contrib.sessions',
    'django.contrib.messages',
    'django.contrib.staticfiles',

    # Local
    'todos.apps.TodosConfig', # new
]
```

If you run `python manage.py runserver` on the command line now and navigate to http://127.0.0.1:8000/[37] you can see our project is successfully installed.

---
[37]http://127.0.0.1:8000/

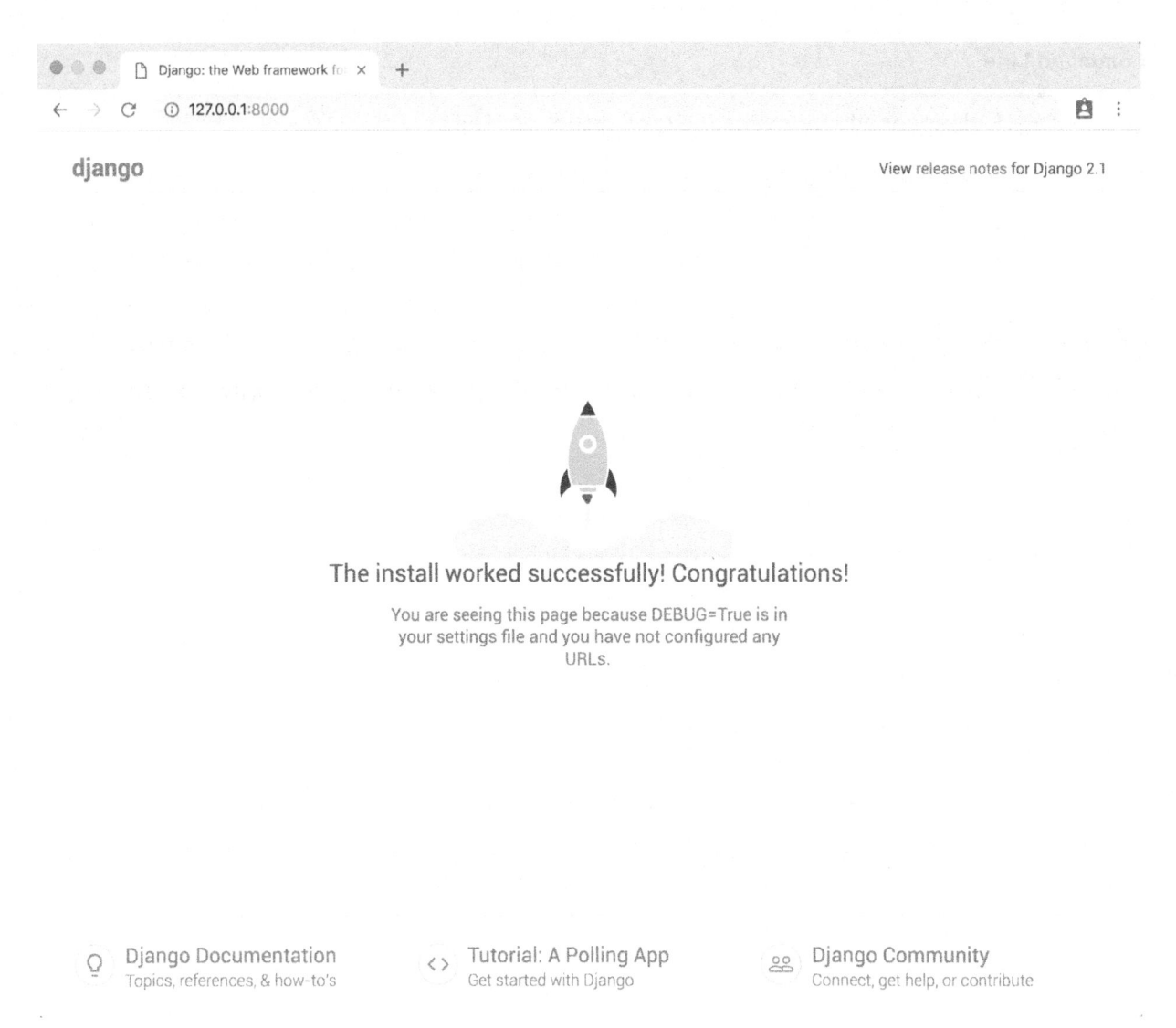

Django welcome page

We're ready to go!

Models

Next up is defining our *Todo* database model within the `todos` app. We will keep things basic and have only two fields: `title` and `body`.

Code

```python
# todos/models.py
from django.db import models


class Todo(models.Model):
    title = models.CharField(max_length=200)
    body = models.TextField()

    def __str__(self):
        return self.title
```

We import `models` at the top and then subclass it to create our own `Todo` model. We also add a `__str__` method to provide a human-readable name for each future model instance.

Since we have updated our model it's time for Django's two-step dance of making a new migration file and then syncing the database with the changes each time. On the command line type `Control+c` to stop our local server. Then run these two commands:

Command Line

```
(backend) $ python manage.py makemigrations todos
(backend) $ python manage.py migrate
```

It is optional to add the specific app we want to create a migration file for—we could instead type just `python manage.py makemigrations`—however it is a good best practice to adopt. Migration files are a fantastic way to debug applications and you should strive to create a migration file for each small change. If we had updated the models in two different apps and then run `python manage.py makemigrations` the resulting single migration file would contain data on *both* apps. That just makes debugging harder. Try to keep your migrations as small as possible.

Now we can use the built-in Django admin app to interact with our database. If we went into the admin straight away our `Todos` app would not appear. We need to explicitly add it via the `todos/admin.py` file as follows.

Code

```python
# todos/admin.py
from django.contrib import admin

from .models import Todo

admin.site.register(Todo)
```

That's it! Now we can create a superuser account to log in to the admin.

Command Line

```
(backend) $ python manage.py createsuperuser
```

And then start up the local server again:

Command Line

```
(backend) $ python manage.py runserver
```

If you navigate to http://127.0.0.1:8000/admin/[38] you can now log in.

---
[38] http://127.0.0.1:8000/admin/

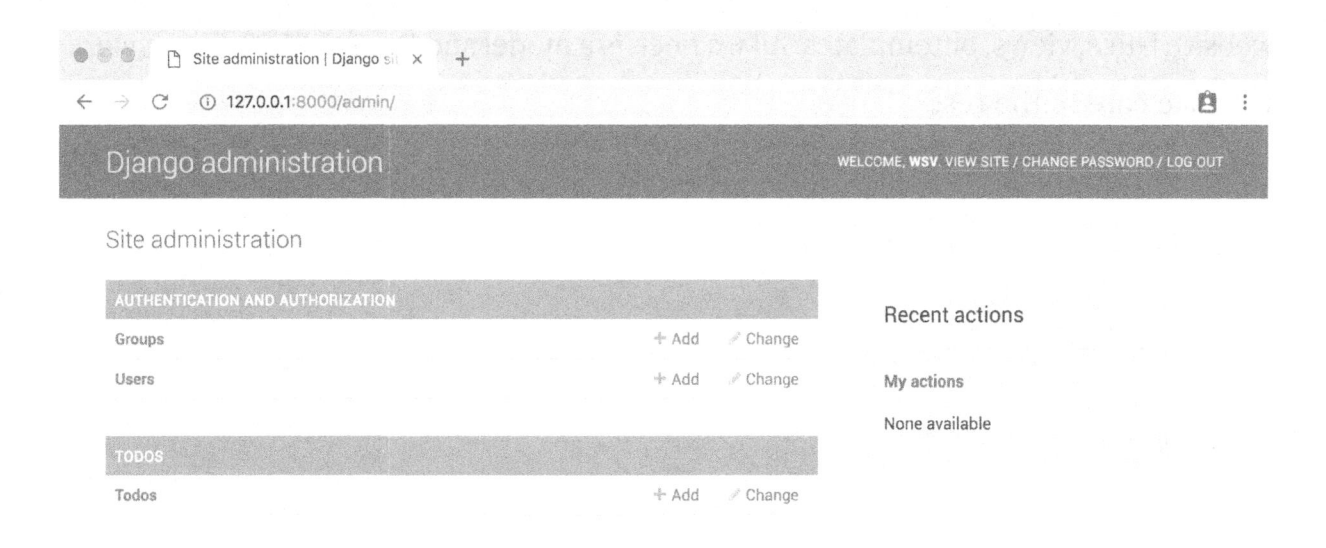

Admin home page

Click on "+ Add" next to Todos and create 3 new todo items, making sure to add a title and body for both. Here's what mine looks like:

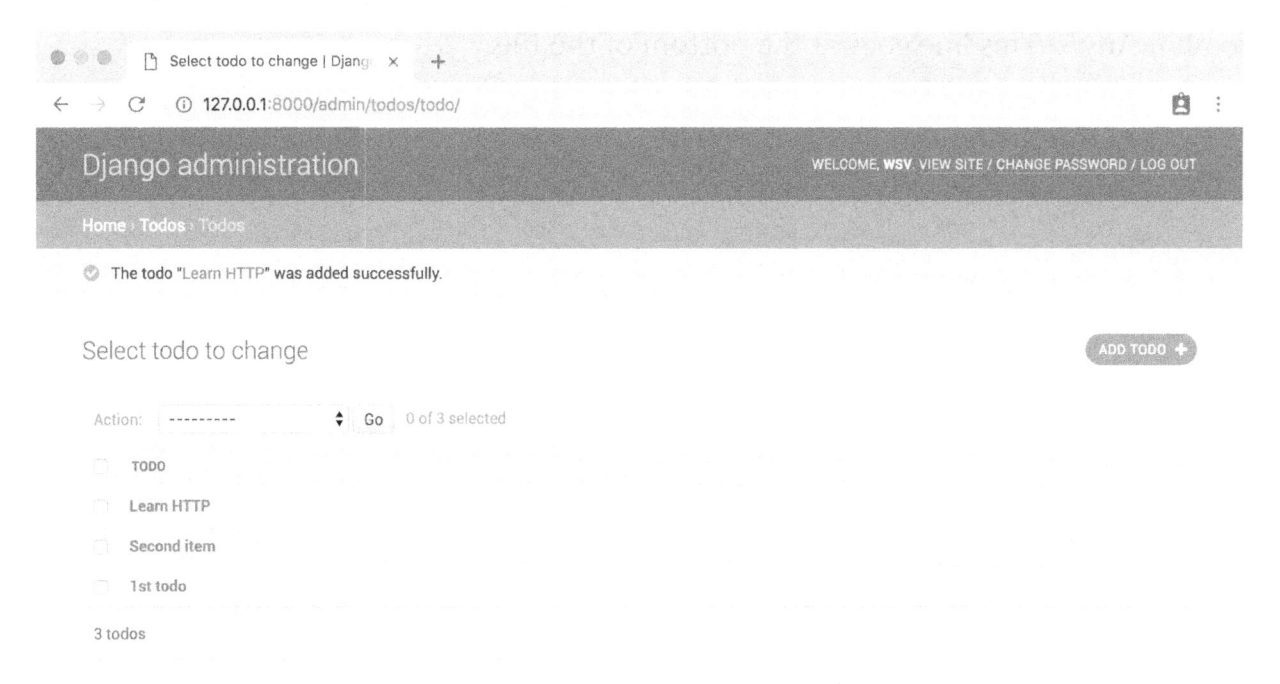

Admin todos

We're actually done with the traditional Django part of our *Todo* API at this point. Since we are not bothering to build out webpages for this project, there is no need for website URLs, views, or templates. All we need is a model and Django REST Framework will take care of the rest.

Django REST Framework

Stop the local server `Control+c` and install Django REST Framework via `pipenv`.

Command Line

```
(backend) $ pipenv install djangorestframework==3.8.2
```

Then add `rest_framework` to our `INSTALLED_APPS` setting just like any other third-party application. We also want to start configuring Django REST Framework specific settings which all exist under `REST_FRAMEWORK`. For starters, let's explicitly set permissions to AllowAny[39]. This line goes at the bottom of the file.

Code

```
# todo_project/settings.py
INSTALLED_APPS = [
    'django.contrib.admin',
    'django.contrib.auth',
    'django.contrib.contenttypes',
    'django.contrib.sessions',
    'django.contrib.messages',
    'django.contrib.staticfiles',

    # 3rd party
    'rest_framework', # new
```

---

[39]http://www.django-rest-framework.org/api-guide/permissions/#allowany

```
    # Local
    'todos.apps.TodosConfig',
]


# new
REST_FRAMEWORK = {
    'DEFAULT_PERMISSION_CLASSES': [
        'rest_framework.permissions.AllowAny',
    ]
}
```

Django REST Framework has a lengthy list of implicitly set default settings. You can see the complete list here[40]. AllowAny is one of them which means that when we set it explicitly, as we did above, the effect is exactly the same as if we had no DEFAULT_PERMISSION_CLASSES config set.

Learning the default settings is something that takes time. We will become familiar with a number of them over the course of the book. The main takeaway to remember is that the implicit default settings are designed so that developers can jump in and start working quickly in a local development environment. The default settings are **not appropriate** for production though. So typically we will make a number of changes to them over the course of a project.

Ok, so Django REST Framework is installed. What next?

Unlike the *Library* project in the previous chapter where we built both a webpage **and** an API, here we are just building an API. Therefore we do not need to create any template files or traditional Django views.

Instead we will update three files that are Django REST Framework specific to transform our database model into a web API: urls.py, views.py, and serializers.py.

---

[40]http://www.django-rest-framework.org/api-guide/settings/

URLs

I like to start with the URLs first since they are the entry-point for our API endpoints. Just as in a traditional Django project, the urls.py file lets us configure the routing.

Start at the Django project-level file which is todo_project/urls.py. We import include on the second line and add a route for our todos app at api/.

Code

```python
# todo_project/urls.py
from django.contrib import admin
from django.urls import include, path # new


urlpatterns = [
    path('admin/', admin.site.urls),
    path('api/', include('todos.urls')), # new
]
```

Next create our app-level todos/urls.py file.

Command Line

```
(backend) $ touch todos/urls.py
```

And update it with the code below.

Code

```python
# todos/urls.py
from django.urls import path

from .views import ListTodo, DetailTodo

urlpatterns = [
    path('<int:pk>/', DetailTodo.as_view()),
    path('', ListTodo.as_view()),
]
```

Note that we are referencing two views—`ListTodo` and `DetailTodo`—that we have yet to create. But the routing is now complete. There will be a list of all todos at the empty string `''`, in other words at `api/`. And each individual todo will be available at its primary key, which is a value Django sets automatically in every database table. The first entry is 1, the second is 2, and so on. Therefore our first todo will eventually be located at the API endpoint `api/1/`.

Serializers

Let's review where we are so far. We started with a traditional Django project and app where we made a database model and added data. Then we installed Django REST Framework and configured our URLs. Now we need to transform our data, from the models, into JSON that will be outputted at the URLs. Therefore we need a serializer.

Django REST Framework ships with a powerful built-in `serializers` class that we can quickly extend with a small amount of code. That's what we'll do here.

First create a new `serializers.py` file in the `todos` app.

Command Line

```
(backend) $ touch todos/serializers.py
```

Then update it with the following code.

Code

```python
# todos/serializers.py
from rest_framework import serializers
from .models import Todo


class TodoSerializer(serializers.ModelSerializer):
    class Meta:
        model = Todo
        fields = ('id', 'title', 'body',)
```

At the top we have imported `serializers` from Django REST Framework as well as our `models.py` file. Next we create a class `TodoSerializer`. The format here is **very** similar to how we create model classes or forms in Django itself. We're specifying which model to use and the specific fields on it we want to expose. Remember that `id` is created automatically by Django so we didn't have to define it in our Todo model but we will use it in our detail view.

And that's it. Django REST Framework will now magically transform our data into JSON exposing the fields for `id`, `title`, and `body` from our `Todo` model.

The last thing we need to do is configure our `views.py` file.

Views

In traditional Django *views* are used to customize what data to send to the templates. In Django REST Framework views do the same thing but for our serialized data.

The syntax of Django REST Framework views is intentionally quite similar to regular Django views and just like regular Django, Django REST Framework ships with generic views for common use cases. That's what we'll use here.

Update the `todos/views.py` file to look as follows:

Code

```python
# todos/views.py
from rest_framework import generics

from .models import Todo
from .serializers import TodoSerializer


class ListTodo(generics.ListAPIView):
    queryset = Todo.objects.all()
    serializer_class = TodoSerializer


class DetailTodo(generics.RetrieveAPIView):
    queryset = Todo.objects.all()
    serializer_class = TodoSerializer
```

At the top we import Django REST Framework's `generics` views and both our `models.py` and `serializers.py` files.

Recall from our `todos/urls.py` file that we have two routes and therefore two distinct views. We will use ListAPIView[41] to display all todos and RetrieveAPIView[42] to display a single model instance.

Astute readers will notice that there is a bit of redundancy in the code here. We essentially repeat the `queryset` and `serializer_class` for each view, even though the generic view extended is different. Later on in the book we will learn about viewsets and routers which address this issue and allow us to create the same API views and URLs with much less code.

But for now we're done! Our API is ready to consume. As you can see, the only real difference between Django REST Framework and Django is that with Django REST Framework we need to add a `serializers.py` file and we do not need a templates file. Otherwise the `urls.py` and `views.py` files act in a similar manner.

Consuming the API

Traditionally consuming an API was a challenge. There simply weren't good visualizations for all the information contained in the body and header of a given HTTP response or request.

Instead most developers used a command line HTTP client like cURL[43], which we saw in the previous chapter, or HTTPie[44].

In 2012 the third-party software product Postman[45] was launched and it is now used by millions of developers worldwide who want a visual, feature-rich way to interact with APIs.

---

[41] http://www.django-rest-framework.org/api-guide/generic-views/#listapiview
[42] http://www.django-rest-framework.org/api-guide/generic-views/#retrieveapiview
[43] https://en.wikipedia.org/wiki/CURL
[44] https://httpie.org/
[45] https://www.getpostman.com/

But one of the most amazing things about Django REST Framework is that it ships with a powerful browsable API that we can use right away. If you find yourself needing more customization around consuming an API, then tools like Postman are available. But often the browsable API is more than enough.

Browsable API

Let's use the browsable API now to interact with our data. Make sure the local server is running.

Command Line

```
(backend) $ python manage.py runserver
```

Then navigate to http://127.0.0.1:8000/api/[46] to see our working API list views endpoint.

---
[46]http://127.0.0.1:8000/api/

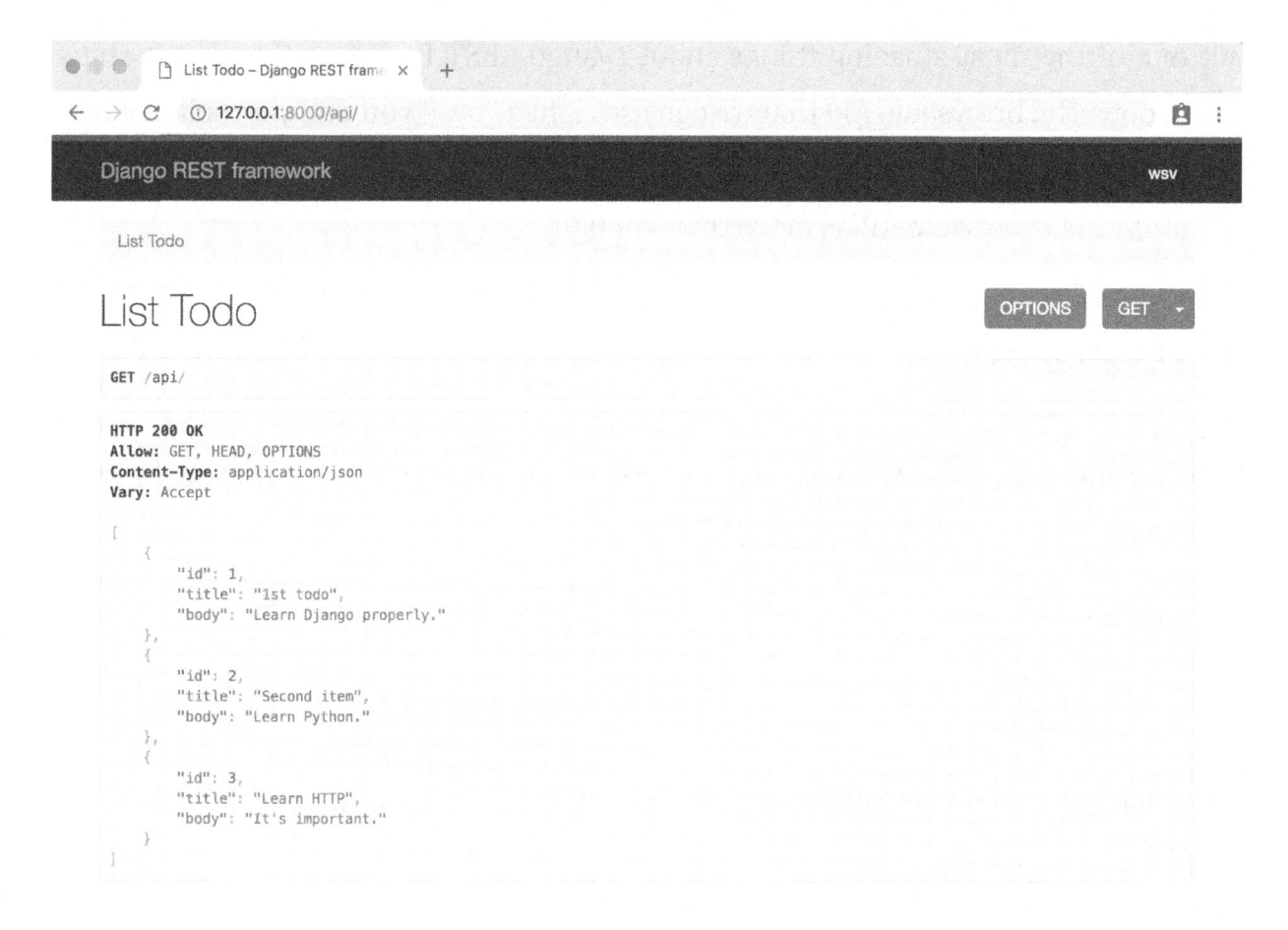

```
  ●●●    ▢ List Todo – Django REST frame ×  +
  ← → C   ⓘ 127.0.0.1:8000/api/                                        👤  ⋮

  Django REST framework                                                   wsv

  List Todo

  List Todo                                              OPTIONS    GET ▾

  GET /api/

  HTTP 200 OK
  Allow: GET, HEAD, OPTIONS
  Content-Type: application/json
  Vary: Accept

  [
      {
          "id": 1,
          "title": "1st todo",
          "body": "Learn Django properly."
      },
      {
          "id": 2,
          "title": "Second item",
          "body": "Learn Python."
      },
      {
          "id": 3,
          "title": "Learn HTTP",
          "body": "It's important."
      }
  ]
```

API List

This page shows the three todos we created earlier in the database model. The API endpoint is known as a **collection** because it shows multiple items.

There is a lot that we can do with our browsable API. For starters, let's see the raw JSON view–what will actually be transmitted over the internet. Click on the "GET" button in the upper right corner and select JSON.

```
  ●●●    ▢ 127.0.0.1:8000/api/?format=js ×  +
  ← → C   ⓘ 127.0.0.1:8000/api/?format=json                            👤  ⋮

[{"id":1,"title":"1st todo","body":"Learn Django properly."},{"id":2,"title":"Second item","body":"Learn Python."},
{"id":3,"title":"Learn HTTP","body":"It's important."}]
```

API JSON

If you go back to our list view page at http://127.0.0.1:8000/api/[47] we can see there is additional information. Recall that the HTTP verb GET is used to read data while POST is used to update or create data.

Under "List Todo" it says `GET /api/` which tells us that we performed a GET on this endpoint. Below that it says `HTTP 200 OK` which is our status code, everything is working. Crucially below that it shows `ALLOW: GET, HEAD, OPTIONS`. Note that it **does not** include POST since this is a read-only endpoint, we can only perform GET's.

We also made a `DetailTodo` view that should show each individual model. This is known as an **instance**. To go to the first instance, navigate to http://127.0.0.1:8000/api/1/[48].

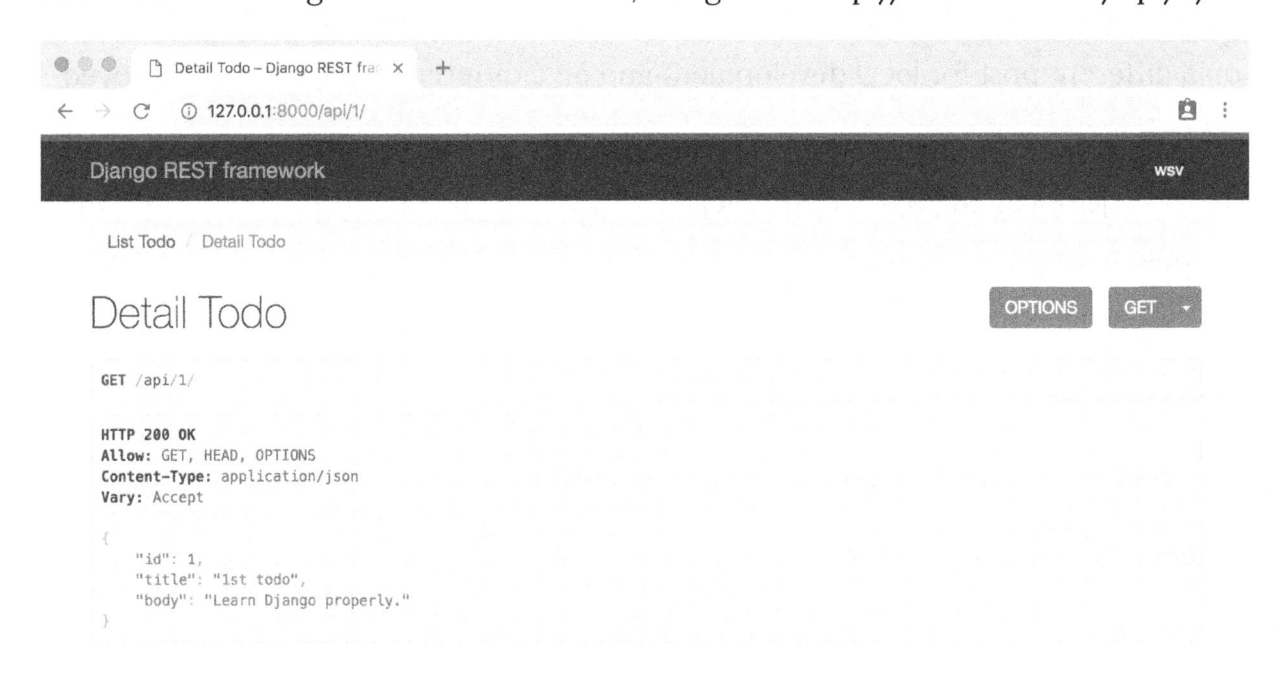

API Detail

You can also navigate to the endpoints for:

- `http://127.0.0.1:8000/api/2`
- `http://127.0.0.1:8000/api/3`

---
[47]http://127.0.0.1:8000/api/
[48]http://127.0.0.1:8000/api/1/

CORS

There's one last step we need to do and that's deal with Cross-Origin Resource Sharing (CORS)[49]. Whenever a client interacts with an API hosted on a different domain (`mysite.com` vs `yoursite.com`) or port (`localhost:3000` vs `localhost:8000`) there are potential security issues.

Specifically, CORS requires the server to include specific HTTP headers that allow for the client to determine if and when cross-domain requests should be allowed.

Our Django API back-end will communicate with a dedicated front-end that is located on a different port for local development and on a different domain once deployed.

The easiest way to handle this--and the one recommended by Django REST Framework[50]--is to use middleware that will automatically include the appropriate HTTP headers based on our settings.

The package we will use is django-cors-headers[51] which can be easily added to our existing project.

First quit our server with `Control+c` and then install `django-cors-headers` with `Pipenv`.

Command Line

```
(backend) $ pipenv install django-cors-headers==2.4.0
```

Next update our `settings.py` file in three places:

- add `corsheaders` to the `INSTALLED_APPS`
- add two new middlewares
- create a `CORS_ORIGIN_WHITELIST`

---

[49]https://developer.mozilla.org/en-US/docs/Web/HTTP/CORS
[50]http://www.django-rest-framework.org/topics/ajax-csrf-cors/
[51]https://github.com/ottoyiu/django-cors-headers/

Code

```python
# todo_project/settings.py
INSTALLED_APPS = [
    'django.contrib.admin',
    'django.contrib.auth',
    'django.contrib.contenttypes',
    'django.contrib.sessions',
    'django.contrib.messages',
    'django.contrib.staticfiles',

    # 3rd party
    'rest_framework',
    'corsheaders', # new

    # Local
    'todos.apps.TodosConfig',
]


MIDDLEWARE = [
    'corsheaders.middleware.CorsMiddleware', # new
    'django.middleware.common.CommonMiddleware', # new
    'django.middleware.security.SecurityMiddleware',
    'django.contrib.sessions.middleware.SessionMiddleware',
    'django.middleware.common.CommonMiddleware',
    'django.middleware.csrf.CsrfViewMiddleware',
    'django.contrib.auth.middleware.AuthenticationMiddleware',
    'django.contrib.messages.middleware.MessageMiddleware',
    'django.middleware.clickjacking.XFrameOptionsMiddleware',
]
```

```
# new
CORS_ORIGIN_WHITELIST = (
    'localhost:3000'
)
```

It's very important that the two new middlewares appear **at the top** of the `MIDDLEWARE` setting. Also note that we're using the domain `localhost:3000` because that's the default port for React, which will be used when we build the front-end. If we later deployed the front-end app to the domain `mysite.com` then we would *also* add that domain to the whitelist setting.

And that's it! Our back-end is now complete. Make sure the server is running as we'll be using it in the next chapter.

Command Line

```
(backend) $ python manage.py runserver
```

Conclusion

With a minimal amount of code Django REST Framework has allowed us to create a Django API from scratch. The only pieces we needed from traditional Django was a `models.py` file and our `urls.py` routes. The `views.py` and `serializers.py` files were entirely Django REST Framework specific.

Unlike our example in the previous chapter, we did not build out any web pages for this project since our goal was just to create an API. However at any point in the future, we easily could! It would just require adding a new view, URL, and a template to expose our existing database model.

An important point in this example is that we added CORS headers and explicitly set only the domain `localhost:3000` to have access to our API. Correctly setting CORS headers is an easy thing to be confused about when you first start building APIs.

There's much more configuration we can and will do later on but at the end of the day creating Django APIs is about making a model, writing some URL routes, and then adding a little bit of magic provided by Django REST Framework's serializers and views.

In the next chapter we will build a React front-end and connect it to our *Todo* API backend.

Chapter 4: Todo React Front-end

An API exists to communicate with another program. In this chapter we will consume our *Todo* API from the last chapter via a React[52] front-end so you can see how everything actually works together in practice.

I've chosen to use React as it is currently the most popular JavaScript front-end library but the techniques described here will also work with any other popular front-end framework including Vue[53], Angular[54], or Ember[55]. They will even work with mobile apps for iOS or Android, desktop apps, or really anything else. The process of connecting to a back-end API is remarkably similar.

If you become stuck or want to learn more about what's really happening with React, check out the official tutorial[56] which is quite good.

Install Node

We'll start by configuring a React app as our front-end. First open up a new command line console so there are now **two consoles open**. This is important. We need our existing Todo back-end from the last chapter to still be running on the local server. And we will use the second console to create and then run our React front-end on a separate local port. This is how we locally mimic what a production setting of a dedicated and deployed front-end/back-end would look like.

---

[52]https://reactjs.org/
[53]https://vuejs.org/
[54]https://angular.io/
[55]https://emberjs.com/
[56]https://reactjs.org/tutorial/tutorial.html

In the new, second command line console install NodeJS[57], which is a JavaScript runtime engine. It lets us run JavaScript outside of a web browser.

On a Mac computer we can use Homebrew[58], which should already be installed if you followed the Django for Beginners instructions[59] for configuring your local computer.

Command Line

```
$ brew install node
```

On a Windows computer there are multiple approaches but a popular one is to use nvm-windows[60]. Its repository contains detailed, up-to-date installation instructions.

If you are on Linux use nvm[61]. As of this writing the command can be done using either cURL:

Command Line

```
$ curl -o- https://raw.githubusercontent.com/creationix/nvm/v0.33.11/\
install.sh
| bash
```

or using Wget

Command Line

```
$ wget -qO- https://raw.githubusercontent.com/creationix/nvm/v0.33.11/\
install.sh | bash
```

Then run:

---

[57]https://nodejs.org/en/
[58]https://brew.sh/
[59]https://djangoforbeginners.com/initial-setup/
[60]https://github.com/coreybutler/nvm-windows
[61]https://github.com/creationix/nvm

Command Line

```
$ command -v nvm
```

Close your current command line console and open it again to complete installation.

Install React

npm[62] is a JavaScript package manager. Like `pipenv` for Python, it makes managing and installing multiple software packages much, much simpler. By default `npm` installs everything locally so there is no risk of collisions between different projects and hence no need for virtual environments as we have in Python.

We will use the excellent create-react-app[63] package to quickly start a new React project. This will generate our project boilerplate **and** install the required dependencies with one command!

Also note that since `create-react-app` will most likely be used to create multiple React apps, we will install it globally with the `-g` flag. If we did not use the `-g` flag then we would have to install `create-react-app` for each new React project.

Command Line

```
$ npm install -g create-react-app
```

Make sure you are in the correct directory by navigating to the Desktop (if on a Mac) and then the `todo` folder.

---

[62]https://www.npmjs.com/
[63]https://github.com/facebookincubator/create-react-app

Command Line

```
$ cd ~/Desktop
$ cd todo
```

Create a new React app called `frontend`.

Command Line

```
$ create-react-app frontend
```

Your directory structure should now look like the following:

Diagram

```
todo
|   ├──frontend
|       ├──React...
|   ├──backend
|       ├──Django...
```

Now change into our `frontend` project and run the React app with the command `npm start`.

Command Line

```
$ cd frontend
$ npm start
```

If you navigate to http://localhost:3000/[64] you will see the create-react-app default homepage.

---
[64] http://localhost:3000/

React welcome page

Mock data

If you go back to our API endpoint you can see the raw JSON in the browser at:

http://127.0.0.1:8000/api/?format=json[65]

Code

```
[
  {
    "id":1,
    "title":"1st todo",
    "body":"Learn Django properly."
  },
  {
    "id":2,
    "title":"Second item",
    "body":"Learn Python."
  },
```

---

[65]http://127.0.0.1:8000/api/?format=json

```
  {
    "id":3,
    "title":"Learn HTTP",
    "body":"It's important."
  }
]
```

This is returned whenever a GET request is issued to the API endpoint. Eventually we will consume the API directly but a good initial step is to mock the data first, then configure our API call.

The only file we need to update in our React app is src/App.js. Let's start by mocking up the API data in a variable named list which is actually an array with three values.

Code

```
// src/App.js
import React, { Component } from 'react';

const list = [
  {
    "id":1,
    "title":"1st todo",
    "body":"Learn Django properly."
  },
  {
    "id":2,
    "title":"Second item",
    "body":"Learn Python."
  },
  {
```

```
    "id":3,
    "title":"Learn HTTP",
    "body":"It's important."
  }
]
```

...

Next we load the list into our component's state and then use the JavaScript array method map()[66] to display all the items.

I'm deliberately moving fast here and if you've never used React before, just copy the code so that you can see how it "would" work to wire up a React front-end to our Django back-end.

Here's the complete code to include in the src/App.js file now.

Code

```
// src/App.js
import React, { Component } from 'react';

const list = [
  {
    "id":1,
    "title":"1st todo",
    "body":"Learn Django properly."
  },
  {
    "id":2,
    "title":"Second item",
```

[66]https://developer.mozilla.org/en-US/docs/Web/JavaScript/Reference/Global_Objects/Array/map

```
      "body":"Learn Python."
    },
    {
      "id":3,
      "title":"Learn HTTP",
      "body":"It's important."
    }
]


class App extends Component {
  constructor(props) {
    super(props);
    this.state = { list };
  }

  render() {
    return (
      <div>
        {this.state.list.map(item => (
          <div key={item.id}>
            <h1>{item.title}</h1>
            <p>{item.body}</p>
          </div>
        ))}
      </div>
    );
  }
}
```

```
export default App;
```

We have loaded `list` into the state of the `App` component, then we're using `map` to loop over each item in the list displaying the `title` and `body` of each. We've also added the `id` as a key which is a React-specific requirement; the `id` is automatically added by Django to every database field for us.

You should now see our todos listed on the homepage at http://localhost:3000/[67] without needing to refresh the page.

1st todo

Learn Django properly.

Second item

Learn Python.

Learn HTTP

It's important.

Dummy data

Note: If you spend any time working with React, it's likely at some point you will see the error message `sh: react-scripts: command not found` while running `npm start`. Don't be alarmed. This is a **very, very common** issue in JavaScript development. The fix is typically to run `npm install` and then try `npm start` again. If that does not work, then delete your `node_modules` folder and run `npm install`. That solves the issue 99% of the time. Welcome to modern JavaScript development :).

---
[67]http://localhost:3000/

Django REST Framework + React

Now let's hook into our *Todo* API for real instead of using the mock data in the `list` variable. In the other command line console our Django server is running and we know the API endpoint listing all todos is located at http://127.0.0.1:8000/api/[68]. So we need to issue a `GET` request to it.

There are two popular ways to make HTTP requests: with the built-in Fetch API[69] or with axios[70], which comes with several additional features. We will use `axios` in this example. Stop the React app currently running on the command line with `Control+c`. Then install `axios`.

Command Line

```
$ npm install axios
```

In the past, developers would add a `--save` flag to `npm` commands to save the dependency in the `package.json` file. You will often see the above command written as `npm install axios --save` as a result. However the most recent versions of `npm` use –save by default[71] so it is no longer necessary to explicitly add the `--save` flag.

Start up the React app again using `npm start`.

Command Line

```
$ npm start
```

Then in your text editor at the top of the `App.js` file import Axios.

---

[68] http://127.0.0.1:8000/api/
[69] https://developer.mozilla.org/en-US/docs/Web/API/Fetch_API
[70] https://github.com/axios/axios
[71] https://blog.npmjs.org/post/161081169345/v500

Code

```
import React, { Component } from 'react';
import axios from 'axios';
...
```

There are two remaining steps. First, we'll use `axios` for our GET request. We can make a dedicated `getTodos` function for this purpose.

Second, we want to make sure that this API call is issued at the correct time during the React lifecycle. HTTP requests should be made using componentDidMount[72] so we will call `getTodos` there.

We can also delete the mock `list` since it is no longer needed. Our complete `App.js` file will now look as follows.

Code

```
// src/App.js
import React, { Component } from 'react';
import axios from 'axios'; // new


class App extends Component {
  state = {
    todos: []
  };


  // new
  componentDidMount() {
    this.getTodos();
  }
```

---

[72]https://reactjs.org/docs/state-and-lifecycle.html

```
// new
getTodos() {
  axios
    .get('http://127.0.0.1:8000/api/')
    .then(res => {
      this.setState({ todos: res.data });
    })
    .catch(err => {
      console.log(err);
    });
}

render() {
  return (
    <div>
      {this.state.todos.map(item => (
        <div key={item.id}>
          <h1>{item.title}</h1>
          <span>{item.body}</span>
        </div>
      ))}
    </div>
  );
}
}

export default App;
```

If you look again at http://localhost:3000/[73] the page is the same even though we no longer have hardcoded data. It all comes from our API endpoint and request now.

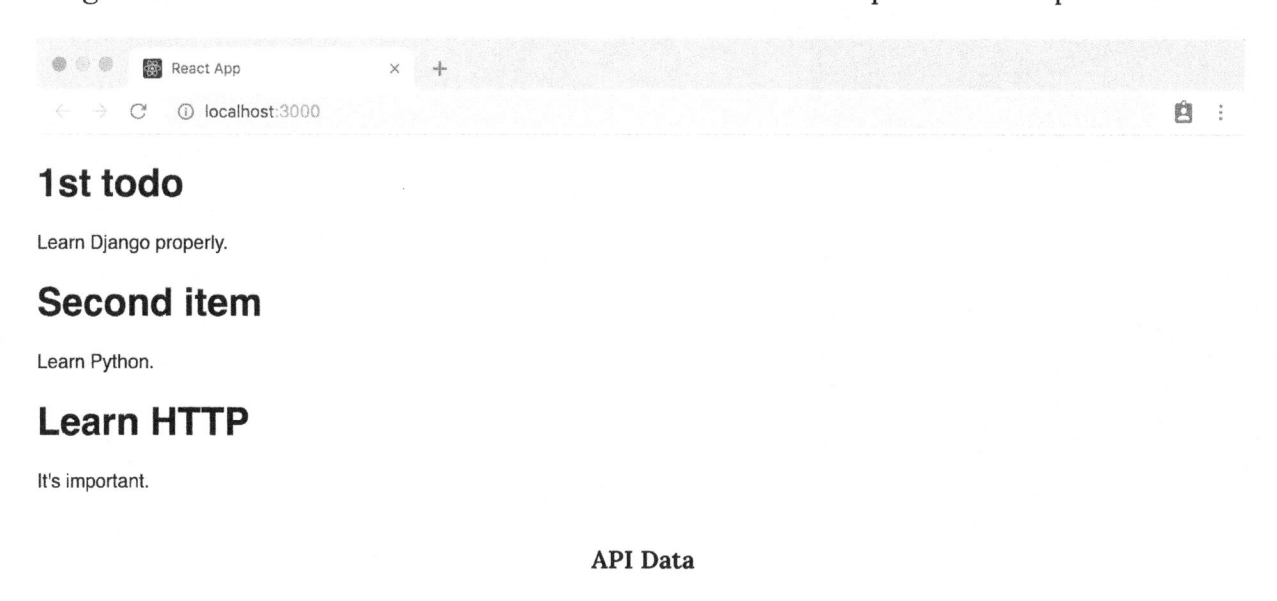

1st todo

Learn Django properly.

Second item

Learn Python.

Learn HTTP

It's important.

API Data

And that is how it's done with React!

Conclusion

We have now connected our Django back-end API to a React front-end. Even better, we have the option to update our front-end in the future or swap it out entirely as project requirements change.

This is why adopting an API-first approach is a great way to "future-proof" your website. It may take a little more work upfront, but it provides much more flexibility. In later chapters we will enhance our APIs so they support multiple HTTP verbs such as POST (adding new todos), PUT (updating existing todos), and DELETE (removing todos).

In the next chapter we will start building out a robust *Blog* API that supports full CRUD (Create-Read-Update-Delete) functionality and later on add user authentication to it so users can log in, log out, and sign up for accounts via our API.

---

[73]http://localhost:3000/

Chapter 5: Blog API

Our next project is a *Blog* API using the full set of Django REST Framework features. It will have users, permissions, and allow for full CRUD (Create-Read-Update-Delete) functionality. We'll also explore viewsets, routers, and documentation.

In this chapter we will build the basic API section. Just as with our *Library* and *Todo* APIs, we start with traditional Django and then add in Django REST Framework. The main difference is that our API endpoints will support CRUD from the beginning which, as we will see, Django REST Framework makes quite seamless to do.

Initial Set Up

Our set up is the same as before. Navigate into a dedicated directory: we'll call ours `blogapi`. Then install Django in a new virtual environment create a new Django project (`blog_project`) and app for blog entries (`posts`).

Command Line

```
$ cd ~/Desktop
$ mkdir blogapi && cd blogapi
$ pipenv install django==2.1
$ pipenv shell
(blogapi) $ django-admin startproject blog_project .
(blogapi) $ python manage.py startapp posts
```

I have shortened the name of the activated virtual environment to (blogapi) here though in reality it will be (blogapi-XXXX) where the XXXX is a random string of characters.

Since we've added a new app we need to tell Django about it. So make sure to add `posts` to our list of INSTALLED_APPS in the `settings.py` file.

Code

```
# blog_project/settings.py
INSTALLED_APPS = [
    'django.contrib.admin',
    'django.contrib.auth',
    'django.contrib.contenttypes',
    'django.contrib.sessions',
    'django.contrib.messages',
    'django.contrib.staticfiles',

    # Local
    'posts.apps.PostsConfig', # new
]
```

Now run `migrate` for the first time to sync our database with Django's default settings and the new app.

Command Line

```
(blogapi) $ python manage.py migrate
```

Model

Our database model will have five fields: `author`, `title`, `body`, `created_at`, and `updated_at`. We can use Django's built-in User model as the author provided we import it on the second line from the top.

Code

```python
# posts/models.py
from django.db import models
from django.contrib.auth.models import User


class Post(models.Model):
    author = models.ForeignKey(User, on_delete=models.CASCADE)
    title = models.CharField(max_length=50)
    body = models.TextField()
    created_at = models.DateTimeField(auto_now_add=True)
    updated_at = models.DateTimeField(auto_now=True)

    def __str__(self):
        return self.title
```

Note that we're also defining what the `__str__` representation of the model should be which is a Django best practice. This way we will see the title in our Django admin later.

Now update our database by first creating a new migration file and then running `migrate` to sync the database with our model changes.

Command Line

```
(blogapi) $ python manage.py makemigrations posts
(blogapi) $ python manage.py migrate
```

Good! We want to view our data in Django's excellent built-in admin app so let's add it to `posts/admin.py` as follows.

Code

```
# posts/admin.py
from django.contrib import admin
from .models import Post


admin.site.register(Post)
```

Then create a superuser account so we can access the admin. Type the command below and enter all the prompts.

Command Line

```
(blogapi) $ python manage.py createsuperuser
```

Now we can start up the local web server.

Command Line

```
(blogapi) $ python manage.py runserver
```

Navigate to http://127.0.0.1:8000/admin/[74] and log in with your superuser credentials.

[74]http://127.0.0.1:8000/admin/

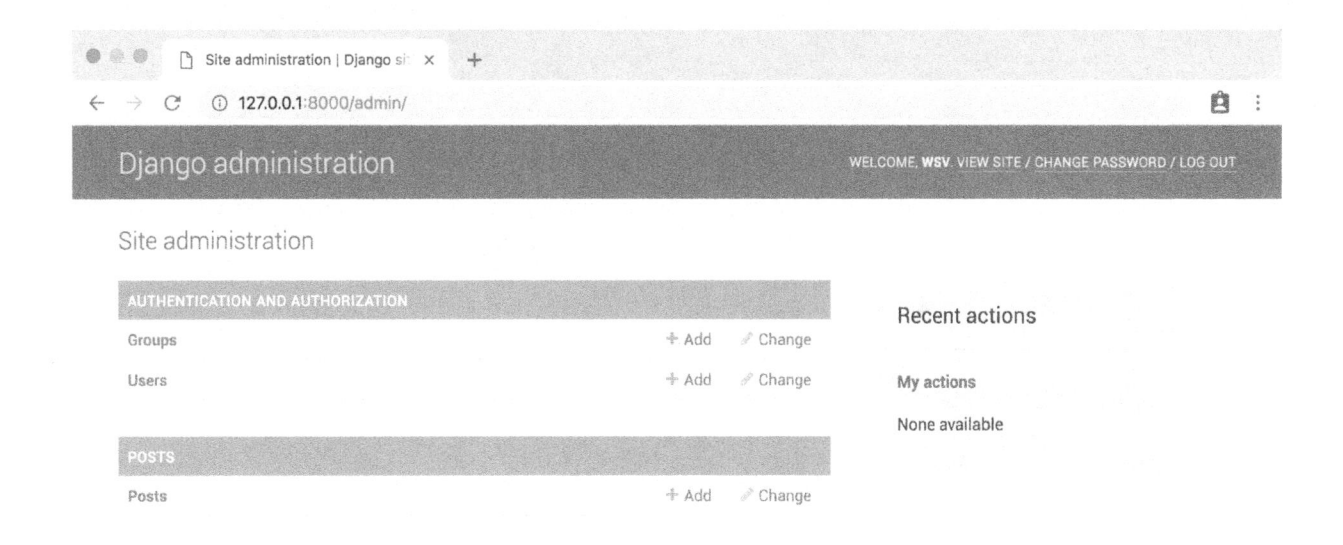

Admin home page

Click on "+ Add" button next to `Posts` and create a new blog post.

Next to "Author" will be a dropdown menu that has your superuser account (mine is called `wsv`). Make sure an author is selected. Add a title and body content then click on the "Save" button.

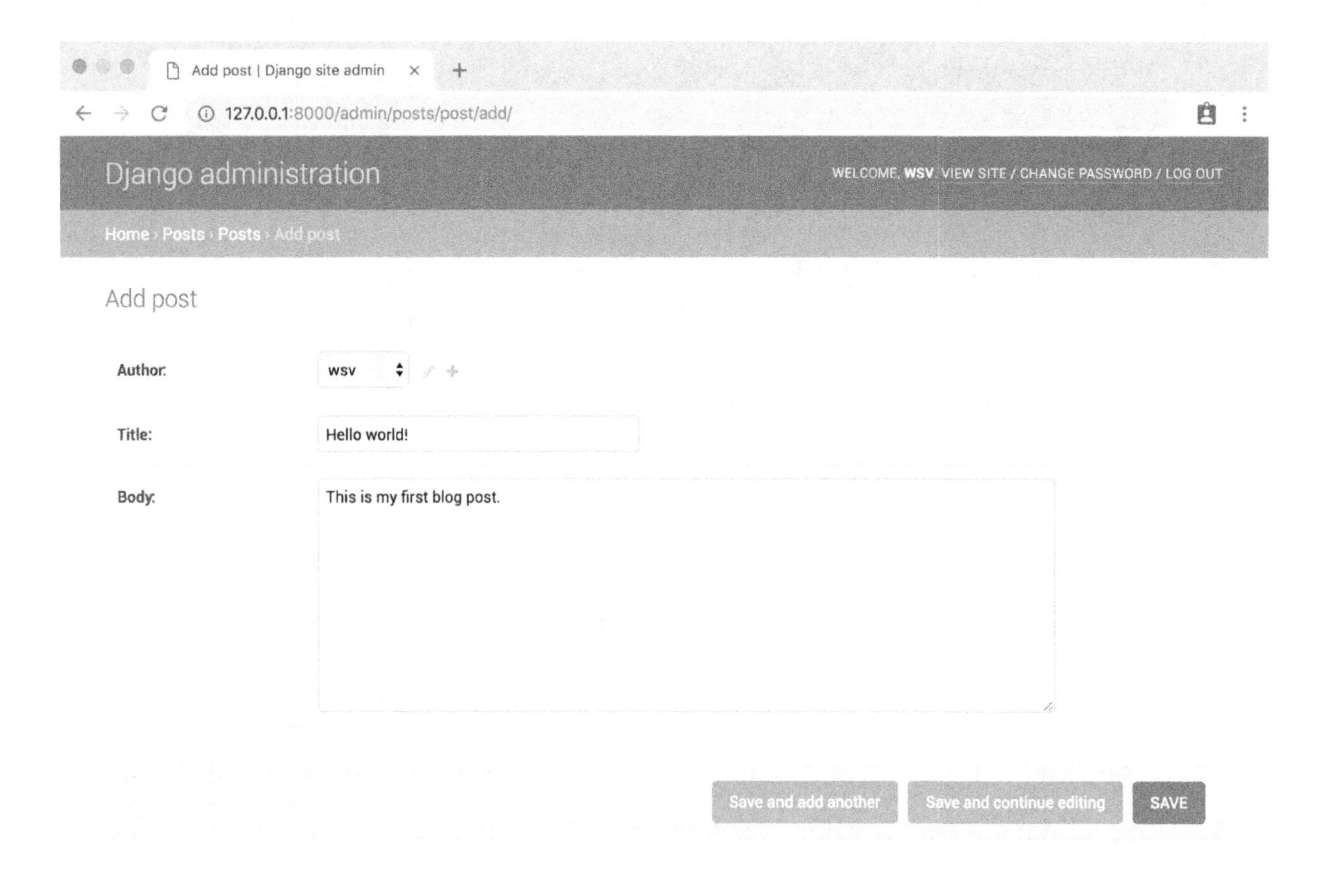

Admin add blog post

You will be redirected to the Posts page which displays all existing blog posts.

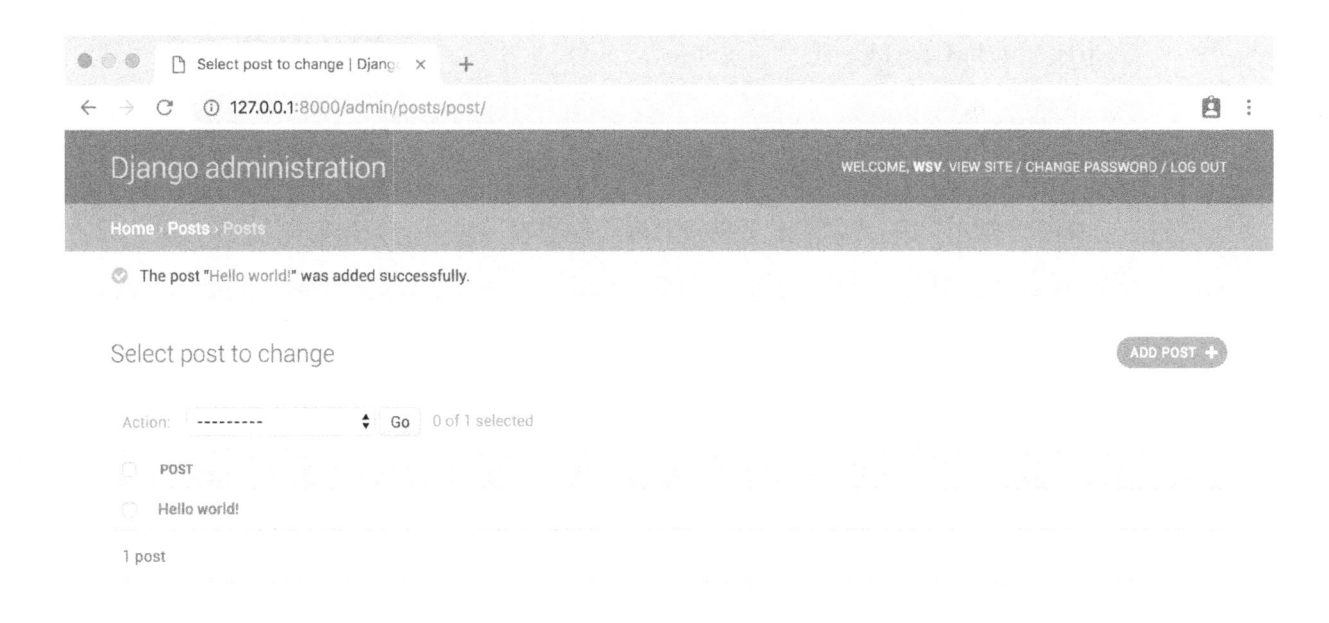

Admin blog posts

Tests

Let's write a basic test for our `Post` model. We want to ensure a logged-in user can create a blog post with a title and body.

Code

```python
# posts/tests.py
from django.test import TestCase
from django.contrib.auth.models import User

from .models import Post


class BlogTests(TestCase):

    @classmethod
```

```python
    def setUpTestData(cls):
        # Create a user
        testuser1 = User.objects.create_user(
            username='testuser1', password='abc123')
        testuser1.save()

        # Create a blog post
        test_post = Post.objects.create(
            author=testuser1, title='Blog title', body='Body content...')
        test_post.save()

    def test_blog_content(self):
        post = Post.objects.get(id=1)
        expected_author = f'{post.author}'
        expected_title = f'{post.title}'
        expected_body = f'{post.body}'
        self.assertEqual(expected_author, 'testuser1')
        self.assertEqual(expected_title, 'Blog title')
        self.assertEqual(expected_body, 'Body content...')
```

To confirm that our tests are working quit the local server Control+c. Then run our tests.

Command Line

```
(blogapi) $ python manage.py test
```

You should see output like the following which confirms everything is working as expected.

Command Line

```
(blogapi) $ python manage.py test
Creating test database for alias 'default'...
System check identified no issues (0 silenced).
.
----------------------------------------------------------------------
Ran 1 test in 0.119s

OK
Destroying test database for alias 'default'...
```

We are done now with the regular Django part of our API. All we really need is a model and some data in our database. Now it's time to add Django REST Framework to take care of transforming our model data into an API.

Django REST Framework

As we have seen before, Django REST Framework takes care of the heavy lifting of transforming our database models into a RESTful API. There are three main steps to this process:

- a `urls.py` file for the URL routes
- a `serializers.py` file to transform the data into JSON
- a `views.py` file to apply logic to each API endpoint

On the command line stop the local server with `Control+c` and use `pipenv` to install Django REST Framework.

Command Line

```
(blogapi) $ pipenv install djangorestframework==3.8.2
```

Then add it to the `INSTALLED_APPS` section of our `settings.py` file. It's also a good idea to explicitly set our permissions which by default in Django REST Framework are configured to `AllowAny`. We will update these in the next chapter.

Code

```python
# blog_project/settings.py
INSTALLED_APPS = [
    'django.contrib.admin',
    'django.contrib.auth',
    'django.contrib.contenttypes',
    'django.contrib.sessions',
    'django.contrib.messages',
    'django.contrib.staticfiles',

    # 3rd-party apps
    'rest_framework', # new

    # Local
    'posts.apps.PostsConfig',
]


# new
REST_FRAMEWORK = {
    'DEFAULT_PERMISSION_CLASSES': [
        'rest_framework.permissions.AllowAny',
    ]
}
```

Now we need to create our URLs, views, and serializers.

URLs

Let's start with the URL routes for the actual location of the endpoints. Update the project-level urls.py file with the `include` import on the second line and a new `api/v1/` route for our `posts` app.

Code

```python
# blog_project/urls.py
from django.contrib import admin
from django.urls import include, path # new


urlpatterns = [
    path('admin/', admin.site.urls),
    path('api/v1/', include('posts.urls')), # new
]
```

It is a good practice to always version your APIs—v1/, v2/, etc—since when you make a large change there may be some lag time before various consumers of the API can also update. That way you can support a v1 of an API for a period of time while also launching a new, updated v2 and avoid breaking other apps that rely on your API backend.

Note that since our only app at this point is `posts` we can include it directly here. If we had multiple apps in a project it might make more sense to create a dedicated api app and then include all the other API url routes into it. But for basic projects like this one, I prefer to avoid an `api` app that is just used for routing. We can always add one later, if needed.

Next create our `posts` app `urls.py` file.

Command Line

```
(blogapi) $ touch posts/urls.py
```

And then include the code below.

Code

```python
# posts/urls.py
from django.urls import path

from .views import PostList, PostDetail

urlpatterns = [
    path('<int:pk>/', PostDetail.as_view()),
    path('', PostList.as_view()),
]
```

All blog routes will be at `api/v1/` so our `PostList` view (which we'll write shortly) has the empty string `''` will be at `api/v1/` and the `PostDetail` view (also to be written) at `api/v1/#` where `#` represents the primary key of the entry. For example, the first blog post has a primary id of 1 so it will be at the route `api/v1/1`, the second post at `api/v1/2`, and so on.

Serializers

Now for our serializers. Create a new `serializers.py` file in our `posts` app.

Command Line

```
(blogapi) $ touch posts/serializers.py
```

The serializer not only transforms data into JSON, it can also specify which fields to include or exclude. In our case, we will include the `id` field Django automatically adds to database models but we will *exclude* the `updated_at` field by not including it in our `fields`.

The ability to include/exclude fields in our API this easily is a remarkable feature. More often than not, an underlying database model will have far more fields than what needs to be exposed. Django REST Framework's powerful serializer class makes it extremely straightforward to control this.

Code

```python
# posts/serializers.py
from rest_framework import serializers
from .models import Post


class PostSerializer(serializers.ModelSerializer):

    class Meta:
        fields = ('id', 'author', 'title', 'body', 'created_at',)
        model = Post
```

At the top of the file we have imported Django REST Framework's `serializers` class and our own models. Then we created a `PostSerializer` and added a `Meta` class where we specified which fields to include and explicitly set the model to use. There are many ways to customize a serializer but for common use cases, such as a basic blog, this is all we need.

Views

The final step is to create our views. Django REST Framework has several generic views that are helpful. We have already used ListAPIView[75] in both the *Library* and *Todos* APIs to create a **read-only** endpoint collection, essentially a list of all model instances. In the *Todos* API we also used RetrieveAPIView[76] for a **read-only** single endpoint, which is analogous to a detail view in traditional Django.

For our *Blog* API we want to list all available blog posts as a read-write endpoint which means using ListCreateAPIView[77], which is similar to the `ListAPIView` we've used previously but allows for writes. We also want to make the individual blog posts available to be read, updated, or deleted. And sure enough, there is a built-in generic Django REST Framework view just for this purpose: RetrieveUpdateDestroyAPIView[78]. That's what we'll use here.

Update the `views.py` file as follows.

Code

```
# posts/views.py
from rest_framework import generics

from .models import Post
from .serializers import PostSerializer


class PostList(generics.ListCreateAPIView):
    queryset = Post.objects.all()
```

---
[75]http://www.django-rest-framework.org/api-guide/generic-views/#listapiview
[76]http://www.django-rest-framework.org/api-guide/generic-views/#retrieveapiview
[77]http://www.django-rest-framework.org/api-guide/generic-views/#listcreateapiview
[78]http://www.django-rest-framework.org/api-guide/generic-views/#retrieveupdatedestroyapiview

```python
    serializer_class = PostSerializer


class PostDetail(generics.RetrieveUpdateDestroyAPIView):
    queryset = Post.objects.all()
    serializer_class = PostSerializer
```

At the top of the file we import `generics` from Django REST Framework as well as our models and serializers files. Then we create two views. `PostList` uses the generic `ListCreateAPIView` while `PostDetail` uses the `RetrieveUpdateDestroyAPIView`.

It's pretty amazing that all we have to do is update our generic view to radically change the behavior of a given API endpoint. This is the advantage of using a full-featured framework like Django REST Framework: all of this functionality is available, tested, and *just works*. As developers we do not have to reinvent the wheel here.

Phew. Our API is now complete and we really did not have to write much code on our own. We will make additional improvements to our API in the coming chapters but it is worth appreciating that it already performs the basic list and CRUD functionality we desire. Time to test things out with the Django Rest Framework's browsable API.

Browsable API

Start up the local server to interact with our API.

Command Line

```
(blogapi) $ python manage.py runserver
```

Then go to http://127.0.0.1:8000/api/v1/[79] to see the Post List endpoint.

[79]http://127.0.0.1:8000/api/v1/

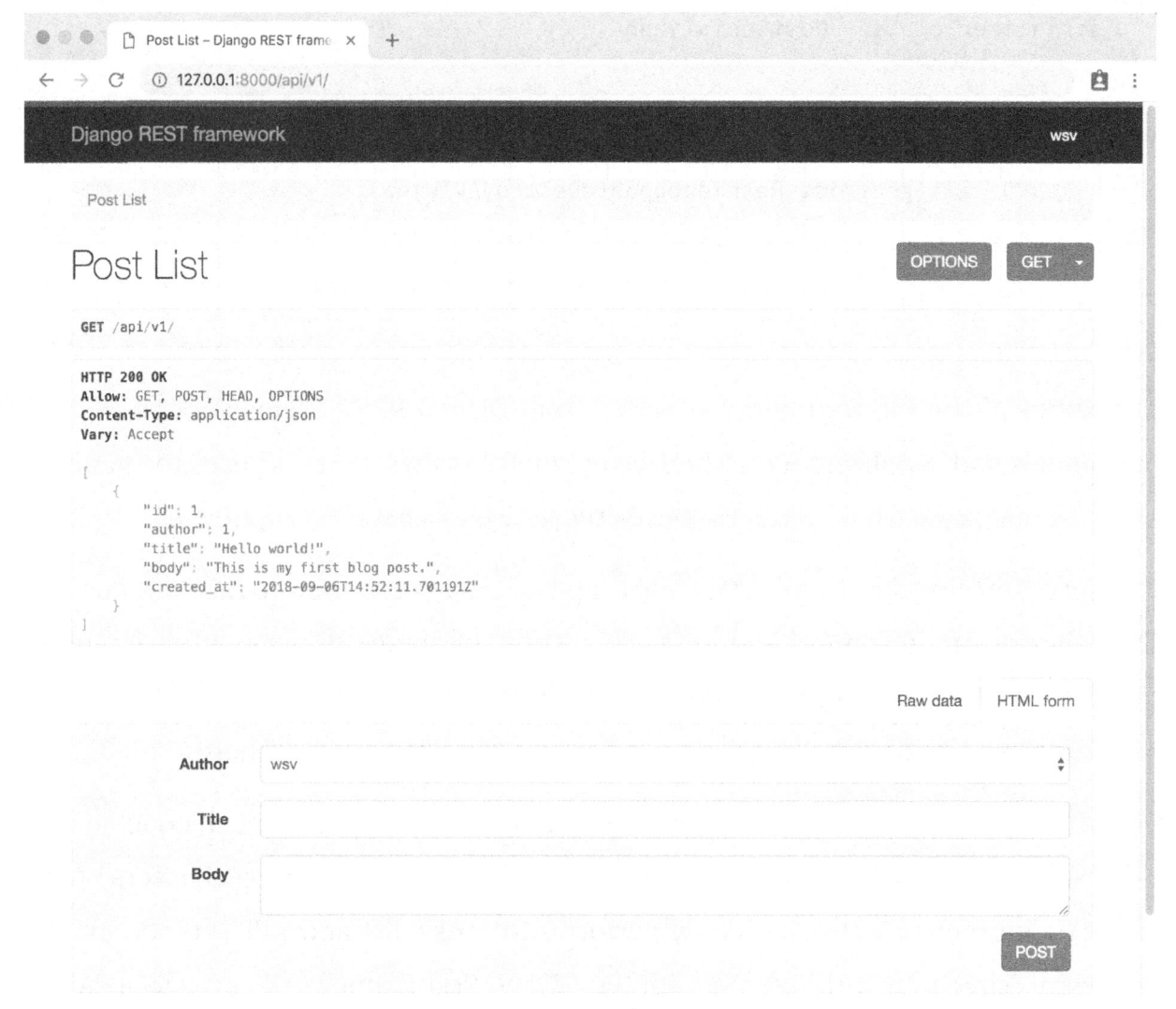

API Post List

The page displays a list of our blog posts–just one at the moment–in JSON format. Note that both GET and POST methods are allowed.

Now let's confirm that our model instance endpoint–which relates to a single post rather than a list of all posts–exists.

Go to http://127.0.0.1:8000/api/v1/1/[80].

---
[80]http://127.0.0.1:8000/api/v1/1/

API Post Detail

You can see in the header that GET, PUT, PATCH, and DELETE are supported but not POST. And in fact you can use the HTML form below to make changes or even use the red "DELETE" button to delete the instance.

Let's try things out. Update our `title` with the additional text `(edited)` at the end. Then click on the "PUT" button.

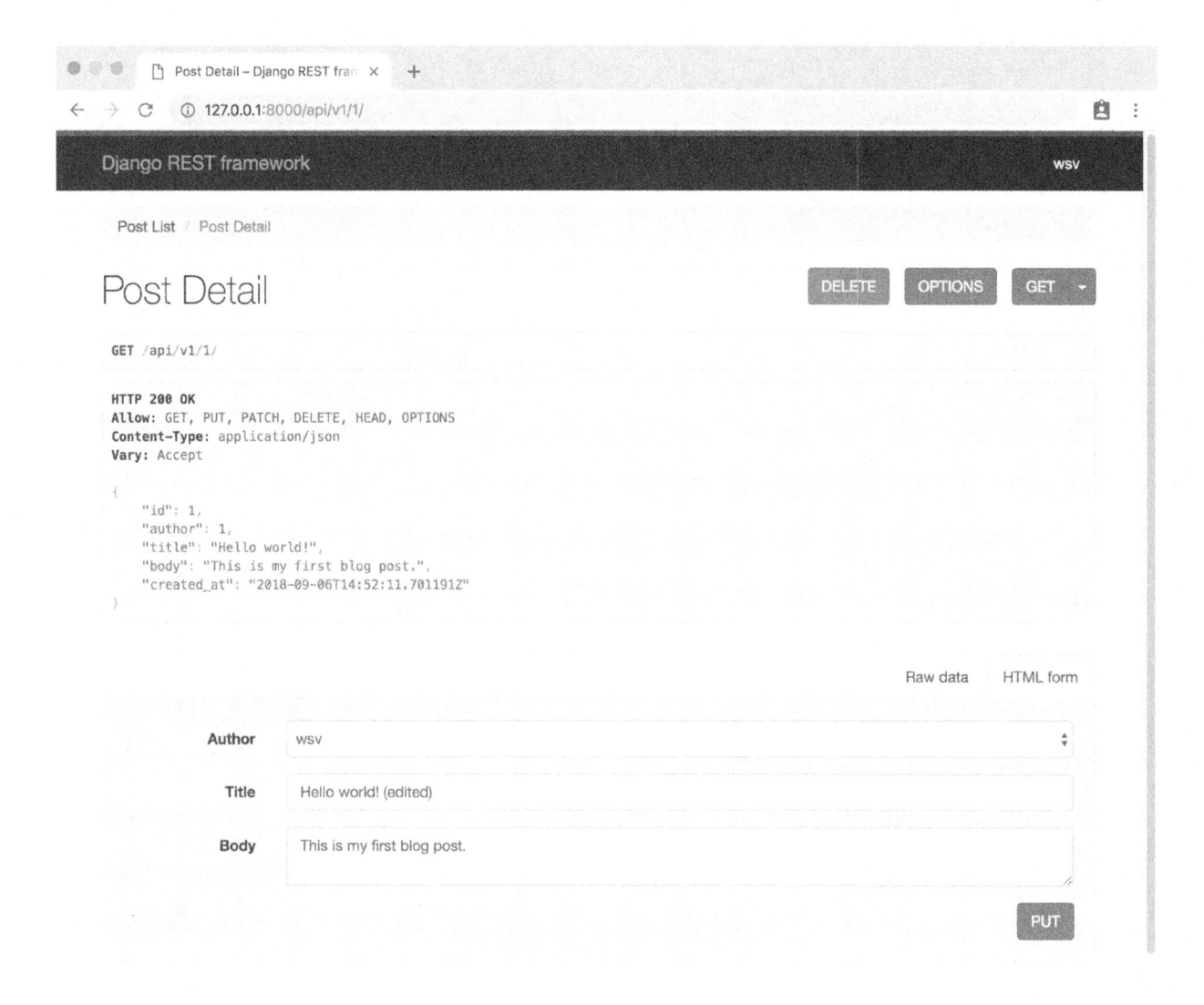

API Post Detail edited

Go back to the Post List view by clicking on the link for it at the top of the page or navigating directly to http://127.0.0.1:8000/api/v1/[81] and you can see the updated text there as well.

---
[81]http://127.0.0.1:8000/api/v1/

API Post List edited

Conclusion

Our *Blog* API is completely functional at this point. However there is a big problem: anyone can update or delete an existing blog post! In other words, we do not have any permissions in place. In the next chapter we will learn how to apply permissions to protect our API.

Chapter 6: Permissions

Security is an important part of any website but it is doubly important with web APIs. Currently our *Blog* API allows anyone full access. There are no restrictions; any user can do anything which is extremely dangerous. For example, an anonymous user can create, read, update, or delete any blog post. Even one they did not create! Clearly we do not want this.

Django REST Framework ships with several out-of-the-box permissions settings that we can use to secure our API. These can be applied at a project-level, a view-level, or at any individual model level.

In this chapter we will add a new user and experiment with multiple permissions settings. Then we'll create our own custom permission so that only the author of a blog post has the ability to update or delete it.

Create a new user

Let's start by creating a second user. That way we can switch between the two user accounts to test our permissions settings.

Navigate to the admin at http://127.0.0.1:8000/admin/[82]. Then click on "+ Add" next to `Users`.

Enter a username and password for a new user and click on the "Save" button. I've chosen the username `testuser` here.

---
[82]http://127.0.0.1:8000/admin/

Add user

First, enter a username and password. Then, you'll be able to edit more user options.

Username: testuser
Required. 150 characters or fewer. Letters, digits and @/./+/-/_ only.

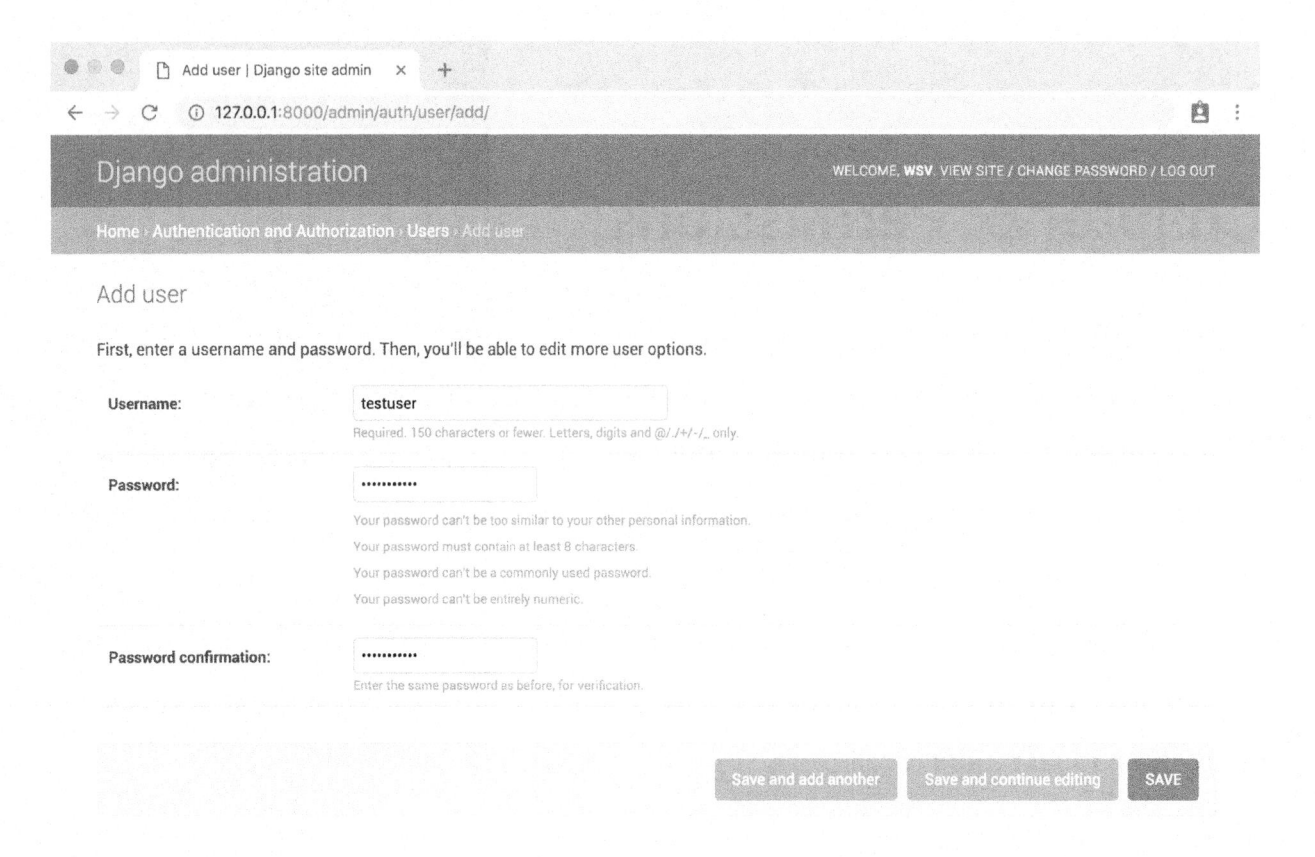

Password: ●●●●●●●●●●
Your password can't be too similar to your other personal information.
Your password must contain at least 8 characters.
Your password can't be a commonly used password.
Your password can't be entirely numeric.

Password confirmation: ●●●●●●●●●●
Enter the same password as before, for verification.

Admin Add User Page

The next screen is the Admin User Change page. I've called my user `testuser` and here I *could* add additional information included on the default `User` model such as first name, last name, email address, etc. But none of that is necessary for our purposes: we just need a username and password for testing.

Admin User Change

Scroll down to the bottom of this page and click the "Save" button. It will redirect back to the main Users page at http://127.0.0.1:8000/admin/auth/user/[83].

---

[83]http://127.0.0.1:8000/admin/auth/user/

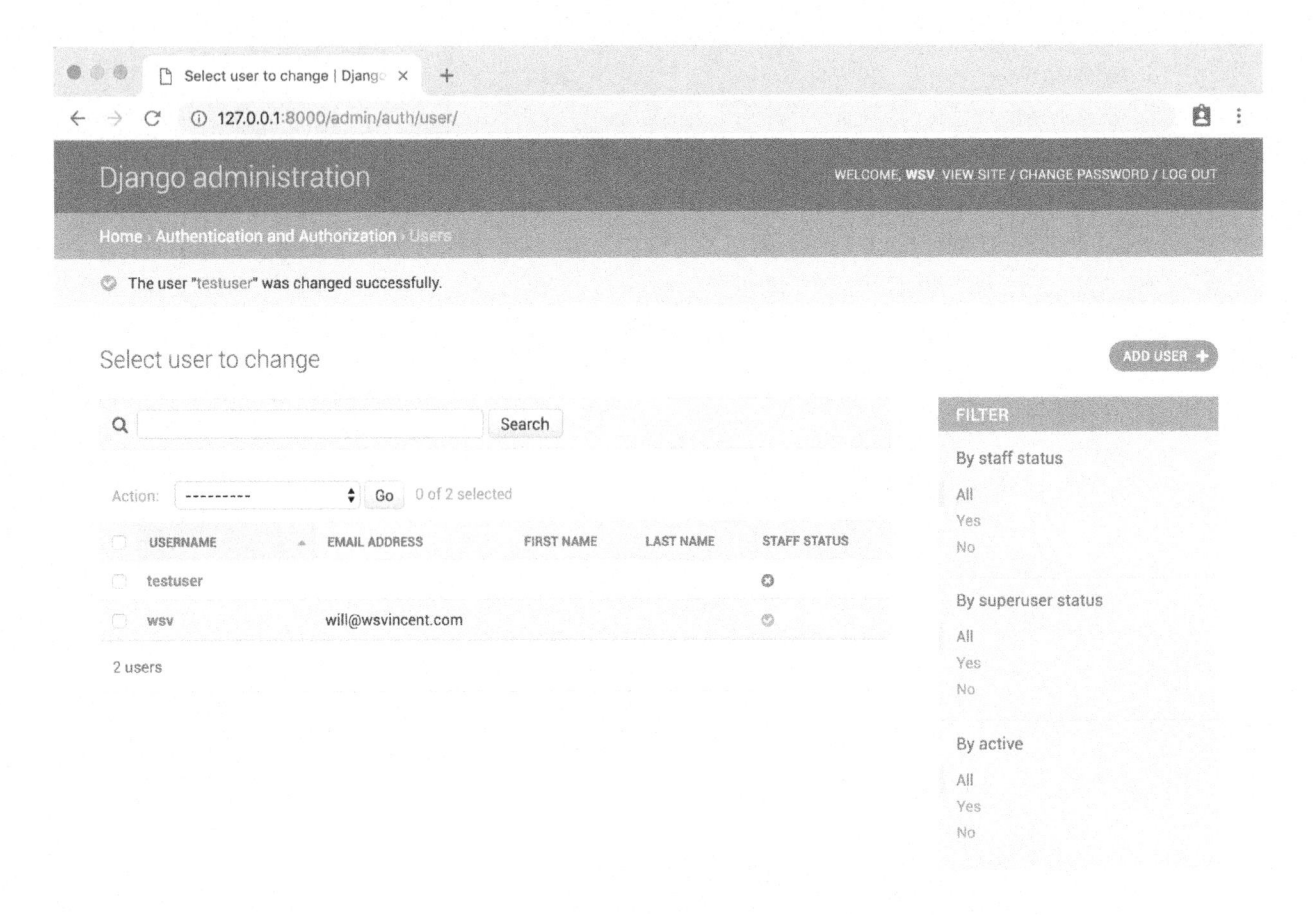

Admin All Users

We can see our two users are listed.

Add log in to the browsable API

Going forward whenever we want to switch between user accounts we'll need to jump into the Django admin, log out of one account and log in to another. Each and every time. Then switch back to our API endpoint.

This is such a common occurrence that Django REST Framework has a one-line setting to add log in and log out directly to the browsable API itself. We will implement that now.

Within the project-level `urls.py` file, add a new URL route that includes `rest_-`

framework.urls. Somewhat confusingly, the actual route specified can be anything we want; what matters is that rest_framework.urls is included *somewhere*. We will use the route api-auth since that matches official documentation, but we could just as easily use anything-we-want and everything would work just the same.

Code

```
# blog_project/urls.py
from django.contrib import admin
from django.urls import include, path

urlpatterns = [
    path('admin/', admin.site.urls),
    path('api/v1/', include('posts.urls')),
    path('api-auth/', include('rest_framework.urls')), # new
]
```

Now navigate to our browsable API at http://127.0.0.1:8000/api/v1/[84]. There is a subtle change: next to the username in the upper right corner is a little downward-facing arrow.

---
[84]http://127.0.0.1:8000/api/v1/

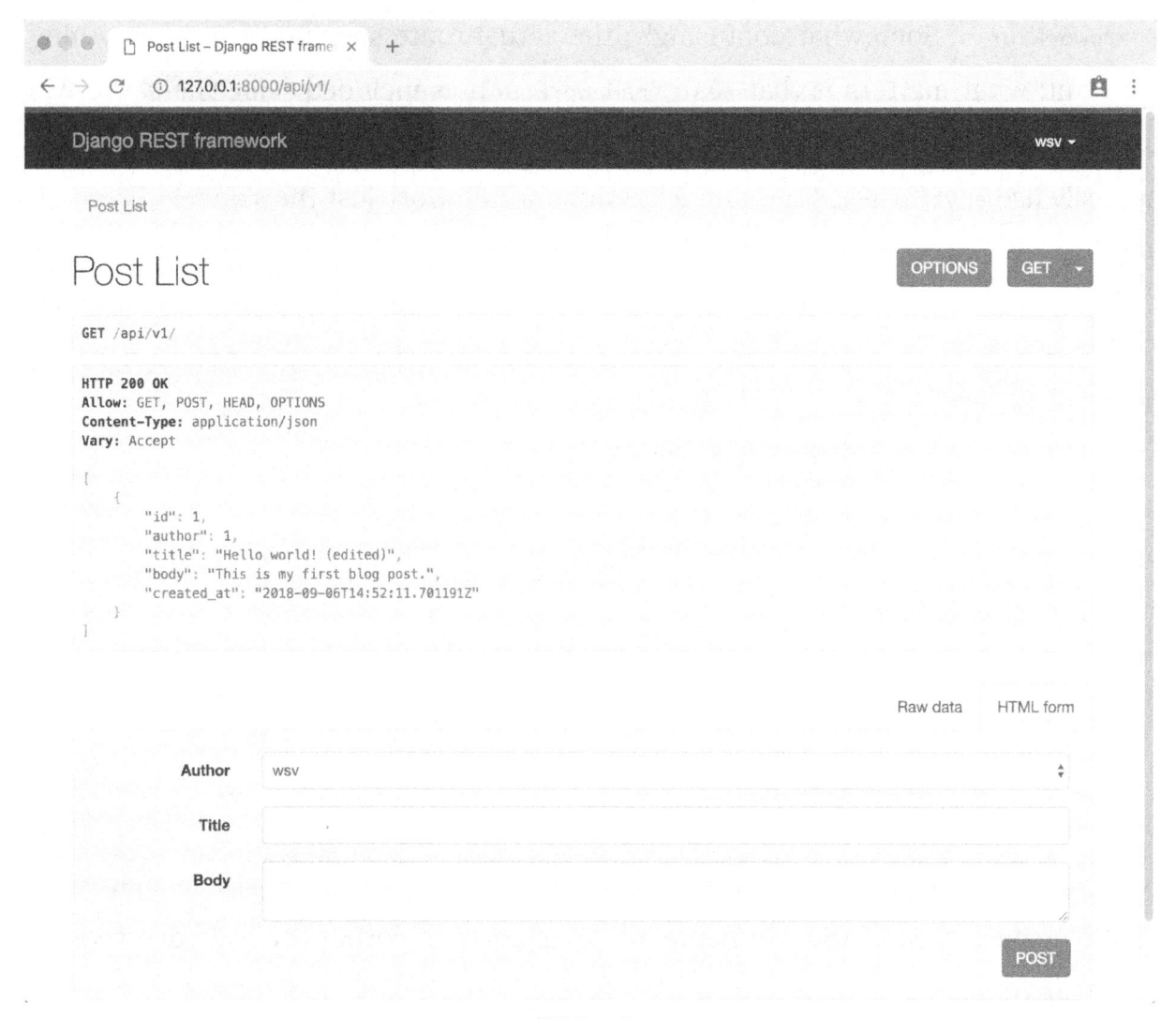

API Log In

Since we are logged in with our superuser account at this point–wsv for me–that name appears. Click on the link and a dropdown menu with "Log out" appears. Click on it.

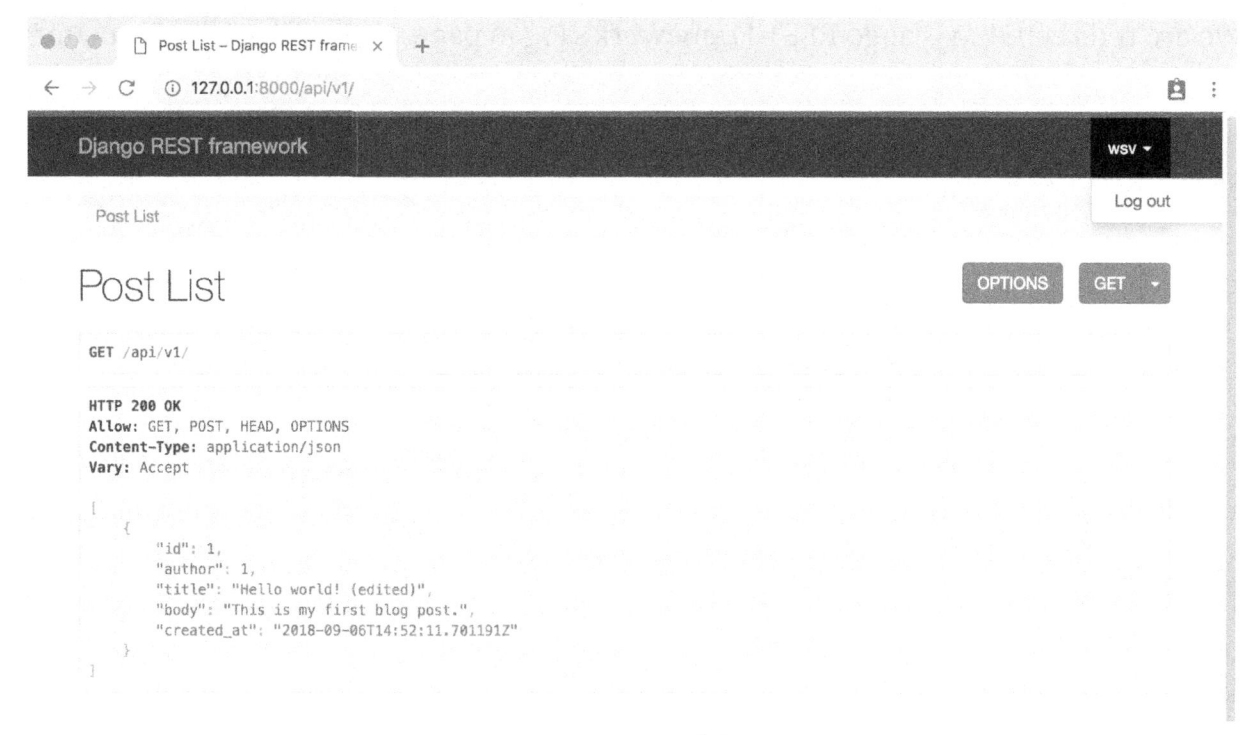

API Log Out Link

The upper righthand link now changes to "Log in." So go click on that.

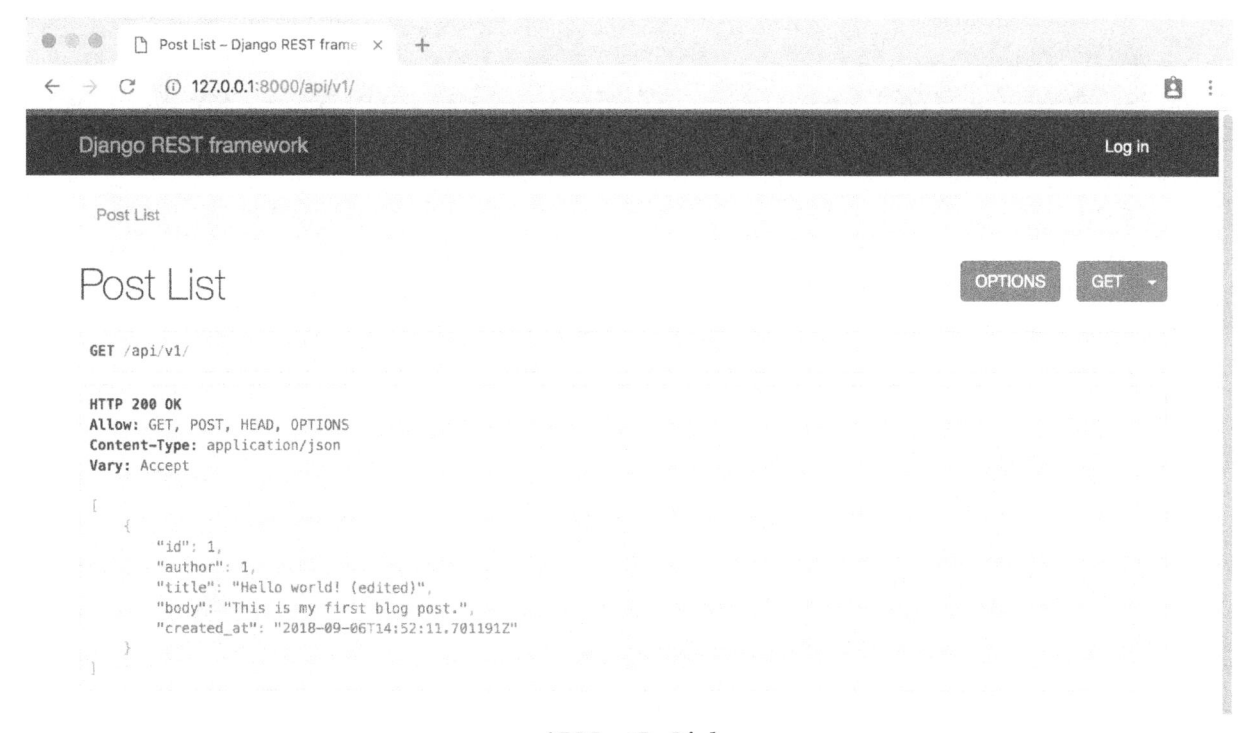

API Log In Link

We are redirected to Django REST Framework's log in page. Use our `testuser` account here.

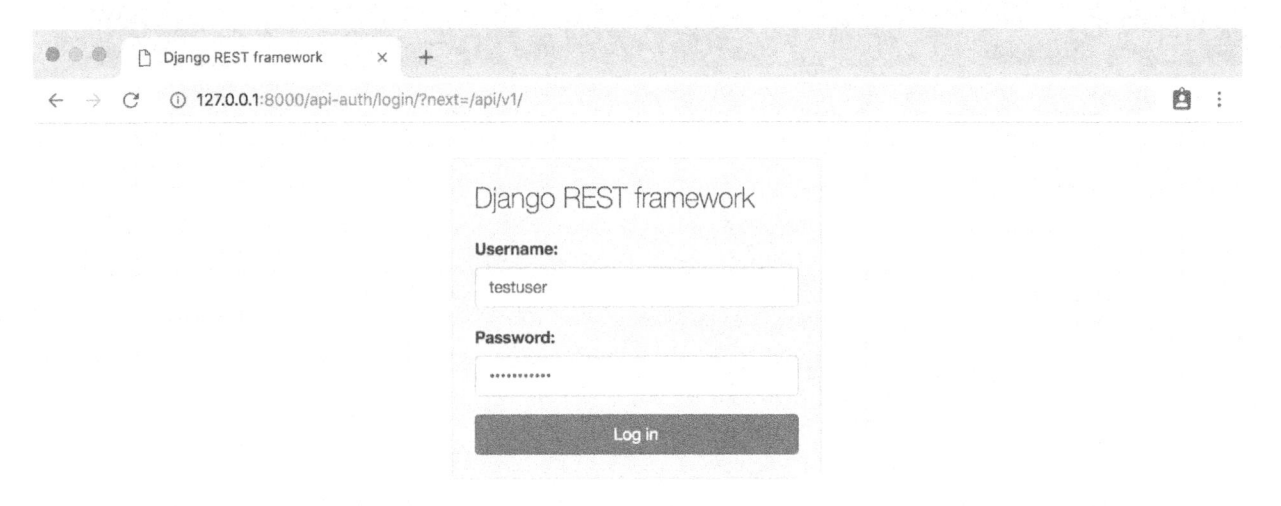

API Log In Page

It will finally redirect us back to the main API page where `testuser` is present in the upper righthand corner.

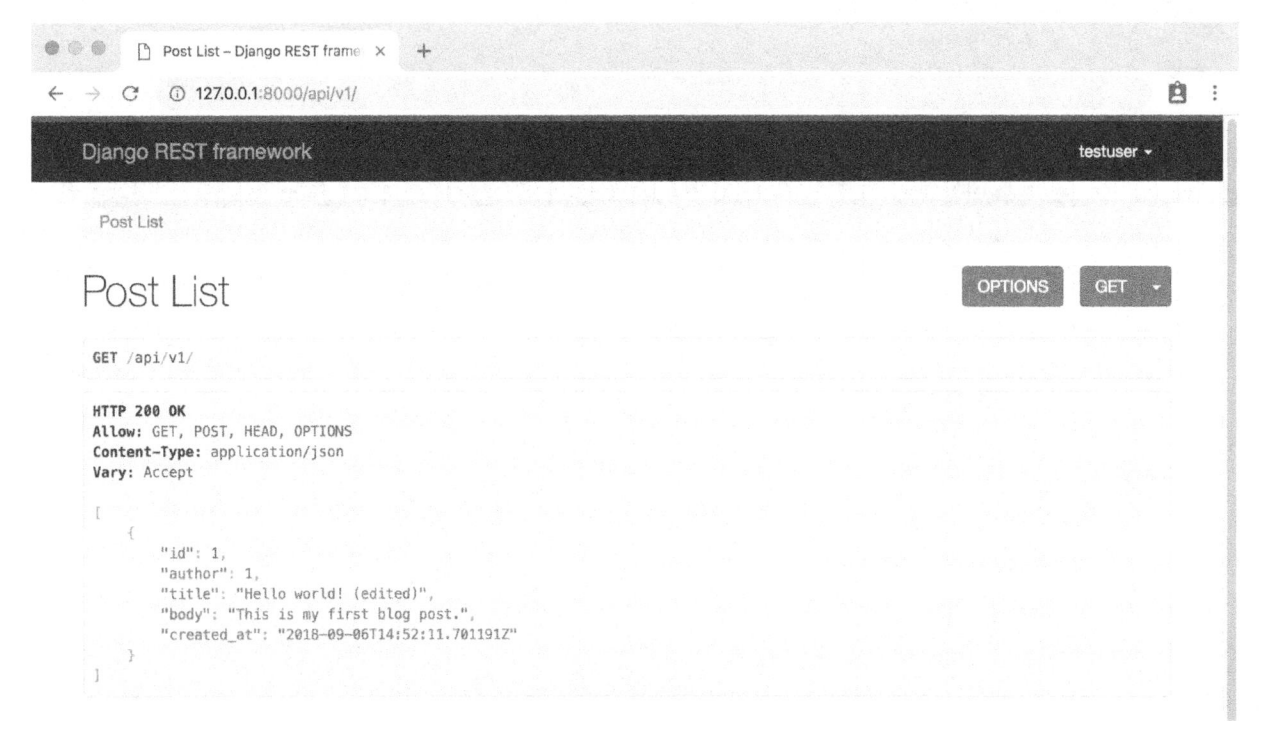

API Log In Testuser

As a final step, log out of our `testuser` account.

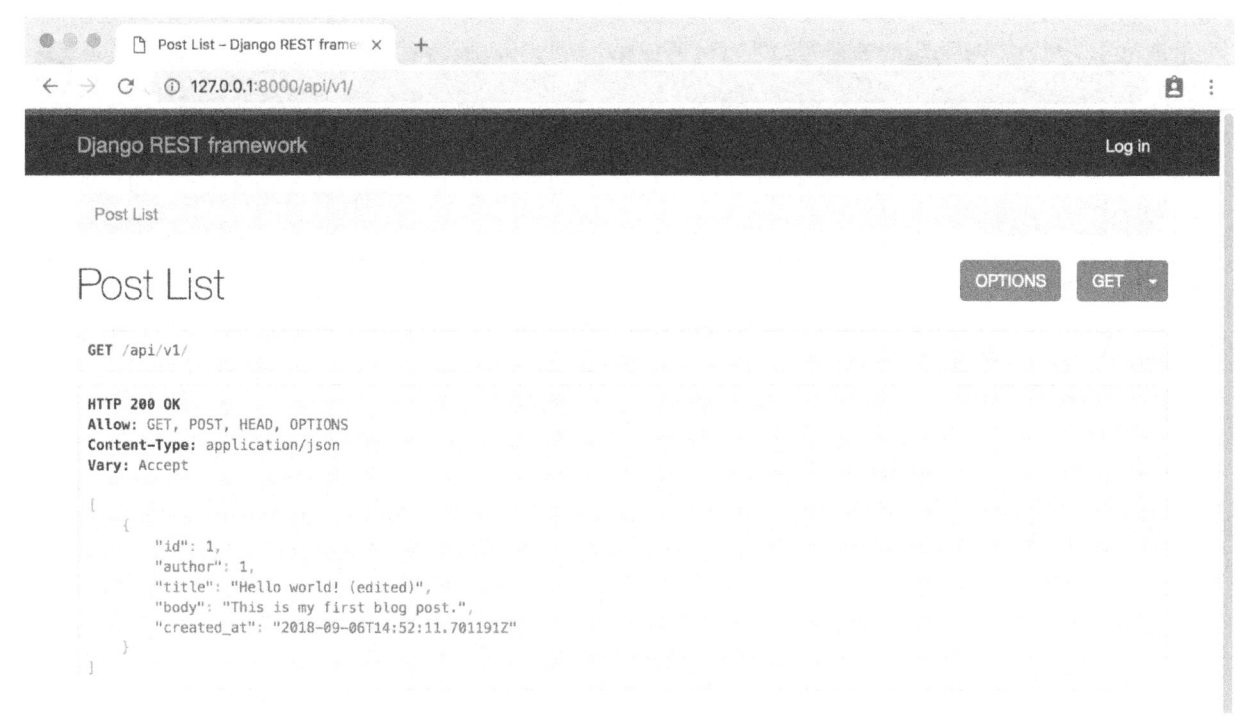

API Log In Link

You should see the "Log in" link in the upper righthand corner again.

AllowAny

Currently an anonymous, non-authorized user can access our `PostList` endpoint. We know this because even though we are not logged-in, we can see our single blog post. Even worse, anyone has full access to create, edit, update, or delete a post!

And on the detail page at http://127.0.0.1:8000/api/v1/1/[85] the information is also visible and any random user can update or delete an existing blog post. Not good.

---
[85]http://127.0.0.1:8000/api/v1/1/

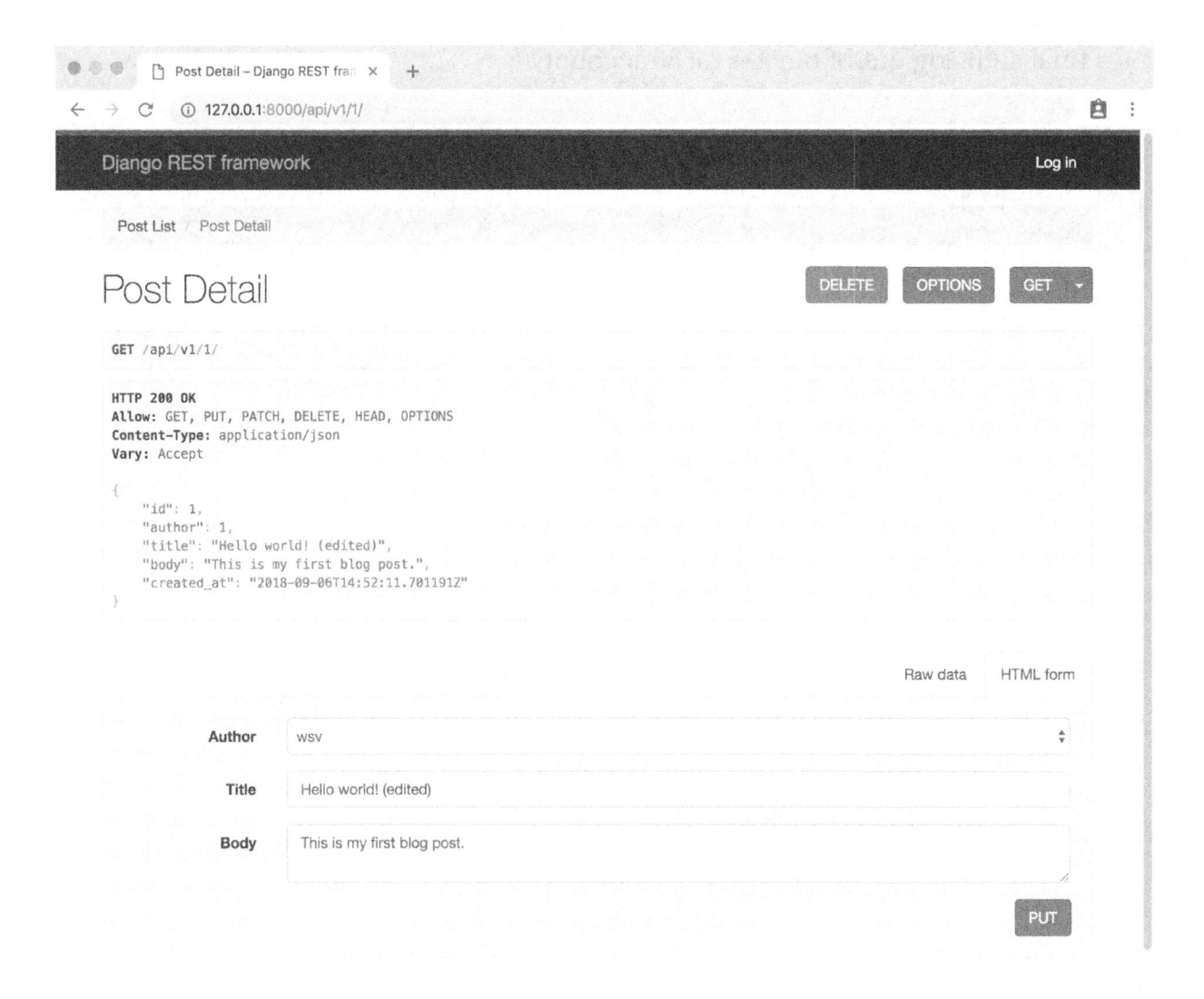

API Detail Logged Out

The reason we can still see the Post List endpoint and also the Detail List endpoint is that we previously set the project-level permissions on our project to `AllowAny` in our `settings.py` file. As a brief reminder, it looked like this:

Code

```
# blog_project/settings.py
REST_FRAMEWORK = {
    'DEFAULT_PERMISSION_CLASSES': [
        'rest_framework.permissions.AllowAny',
    ]
}
```

View-Level Permissions

What we want now is to restrict API access to authenticated users. There are multiple places we could do this–project-level, view-level, or object-level–but since we only have two views at the moment let's start there and add permissions to each of them.

In your `posts/views.py` file, import `permissions` at the top from Django REST Framework and then add a `permission_classes` field to each view.

Code

```
# posts/views.py
from rest_framework import generics, permissions  # new

from .models import Post
from .serializers import PostSerializer


class PostList(generics.ListCreateAPIView):
    permission_classes = (permissions.IsAuthenticated,)  # new
    queryset = Post.objects.all()
    serializer_class = PostSerializer
```

```python
class PostDetail(generics.RetrieveUpdateDestroyAPIView):
    permission_classes = (permissions.IsAuthenticated,)  # new
    queryset = Post.objects.all()
    serializer_class = PostSerializer
```

That's all we need. Refresh the browsable API at http://127.0.0.1:8000/api/v1/[86]. Look what happened!

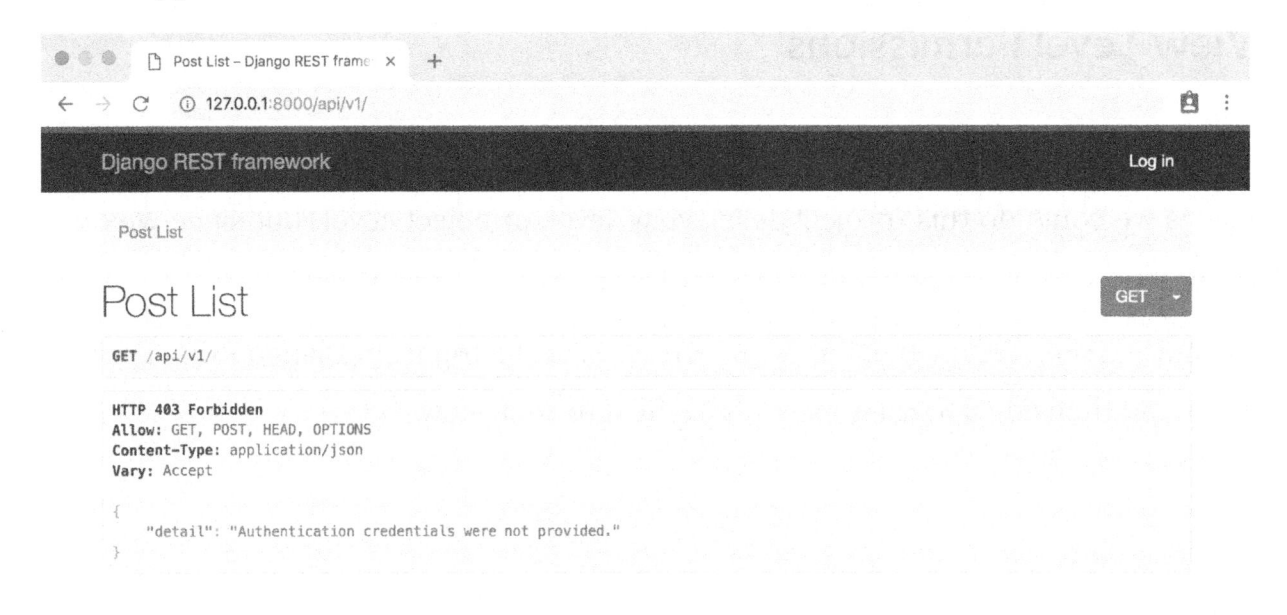

API Post List Logged Out

We no longer see our Post List page. Instead we are greeted with an unfriendly `HTTP 403 Forbidden` status code since we are not logged in. And there are no forms in the browsable API to edit the data since we don't have permission.

If you use the URL for Post Detail http://127.0.0.1:8000/api/v1/1/[87] you will see a similar message and also no available forms for edits.

---
[86]http://127.0.0.1:8000/api/v1/
[87]http://127.0.0.1:8000/api/v1/1/

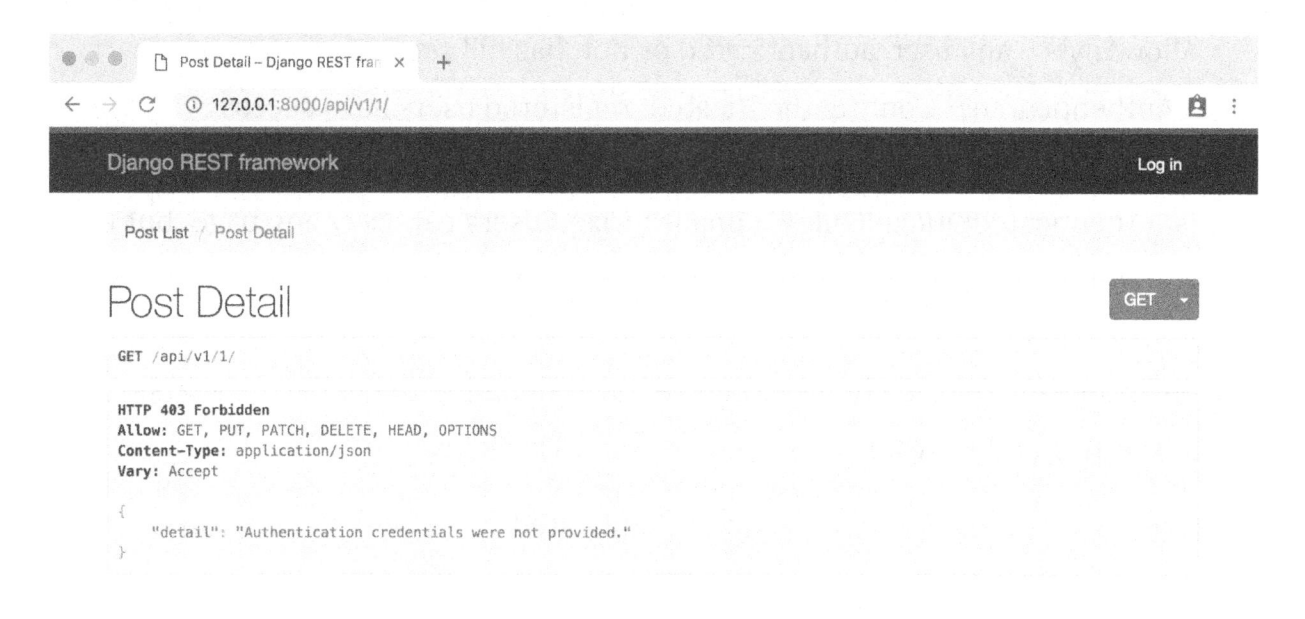

API Detail Logged Out

Therefore at this point only logged-in users can view our API. If you log back in with *either* your superuser or `testuser` account the API endpoints will be accessible.

But think about what happens as the API grows in complexity. It's likely we will have many more views and endpoints in the future. Adding a dedicated `permission_classes` to each view seems repetitive if we want to set the same permissions setting across our entire API.

Wouldn't it be better to change our permissions once, ideally at the project-level, rather than doing it for each and every view?

Project-Level Permissions

You should be nodding your head yes at this point. It is a much simpler and safer approach to set a strict permissions policy at the project-level and loosen it as needed at the view level. This is what we will do.

Fortunately Django REST Framework ships with a number of built-in project-level permissions settings we can use, including:

- AllowAny[88] - any user, authenticated or not, has full access
- IsAuthenticated[89] - only authenticated, registered users have access
- IsAdminUser[90] - only admins/superusers have access
- IsAuthenticatedOrReadOnly[91] - unauthorized users can view any page, but only authenticated users have write, edit, or delete privileges

Implementing any of these four settings requires updating the DEFAULT_PERMISSION_CLASSES setting and refreshing our web browser. That's it!

Let's switch to IsAuthenticated so only authenticated, or logged in, users can view the API.

Update the blog_project/settings.py file as follows:

Code

```
# blog_project/settings.py
REST_FRAMEWORK = {
    'DEFAULT_PERMISSION_CLASSES': [
        'rest_framework.permissions.IsAuthenticated', # new
    ]
}
```

Now go back into the views.py file and delete the permissions changes we just made.

---

[88]http://www.django-rest-framework.org/api-guide/permissions/#allowany
[89]http://www.django-rest-framework.org/api-guide/permissions/#isauthenticated
[90]http://www.django-rest-framework.org/api-guide/permissions/#isadminuser
[91]http://www.django-rest-framework.org/api-guide/permissions/#isauthenticatedorreadonly

Code

```python
# posts/views.py
from rest_framework import generics

from .models import Post
from .serializers import PostSerializer


class PostList(generics.ListCreateAPIView):
    queryset = Post.objects.all()
    serializer_class = PostSerializer


class PostDetail(generics.RetrieveUpdateDestroyAPIView):
    queryset = Post.objects.all()
    serializer_class = PostSerializer
```

If you refresh the Post List and Detail List API pages you will still see the same 403 status code. We have now required all users to authenticate before they can access the API, but we can always make additional view-level changes as needed, too.

Custom permissions

Time for our first custom permission. As a brief recap of where we are now: we have two users, `testuser` and the superuser account. There is one blog post in our database, which is written by the superuser.

We want only the author of a specific blog post to be able to edit or delete it; otherwise the blog post should be read-only. So the superuser account should have full CRUD access to the individual blog instance, but the regular user `testuser` should not.

Stop the local server with `Control+c` and create a new `permissions.py` file in our `posts` app.

Command Line

```
(blogapi) $ touch posts/permissions.py
```

Internally, Django REST Framework relies on a `BasePermission` class from which all other permission classes inherit. That means the built-in permissions settings like `AllowAny`, `IsAuthenticated`, and others extend it. Here is the actual source code which is available on Github[92]:

Code

```python
class BasePermission(object):
    """
    A base class from which all permission classes should inherit.
    """

    def has_permission(self, request, view):
        """
        Return `True` if permission is granted, `False` otherwise.
        """
        return True

    def has_object_permission(self, request, view, obj):
        """
        Return `True` if permission is granted, `False` otherwise.
        """
        return True
```

---
[92]https://github.com/encode/django-rest-framework

To create our own custom permission, we will override the `has_object_permission` method. Specifically we want to allow read-only for all requests but for any write requests, such as edit or delete, the author must be the same as the current logged-in user.

Here is what our `posts/permissions.py` file looks like.

Code

```python
# posts/permissions.py
from rest_framework import permissions


class IsAuthorOrReadOnly(permissions.BasePermission):

    def has_object_permission(self, request, view, obj):
        # Read-only permissions are allowed for any request
        if request.method in permissions.SAFE_METHODS:
            return True

        # Write permissions are only allowed to the author of a post
        return obj.author == request.user
```

We import `permissions` at the top and then create a custom class `IsAuthorOrReadOnly` which extends `BasePermission`. Then we override `has_object_permission`. If a request contains HTTP verbs included in `SAFE_METHODS`–a tuple containing `GET`, `OPTIONS`, and `HEAD`–then it is a read-only request and permission is granted.

Otherwise the request is for a write of some kind, which means updating the API resource so either create, delete, or edit functionality. In that case, we check if the author of the object in question, which is our blog post `obj.author` matches the user making the request `request.user`.

Back in the `views.py` file we should import `IsAuthorOrReadOnly` and then we can add `permission_classes` for `PostDetail`.

Code

```python
# posts/views.py
from rest_framework import generics

from .models import Post
from .permissions import IsAuthorOrReadOnly # new
from .serializers import PostSerializer


class PostList(generics.ListCreateAPIView):
    queryset = Post.objects.all()
    serializer_class = PostSerializer


class PostDetail(generics.RetrieveUpdateDestroyAPIView):
    permission_classes = (IsAuthorOrReadOnly,) # new
    queryset = Post.objects.all()
    serializer_class = PostSerializer
```

And we're done. Let's test things out. Navigate to the Post Detail page. Make sure you are logged-in with your superuser account, who is the author of the post. So it will be visible in the upper righthand corner of the page.

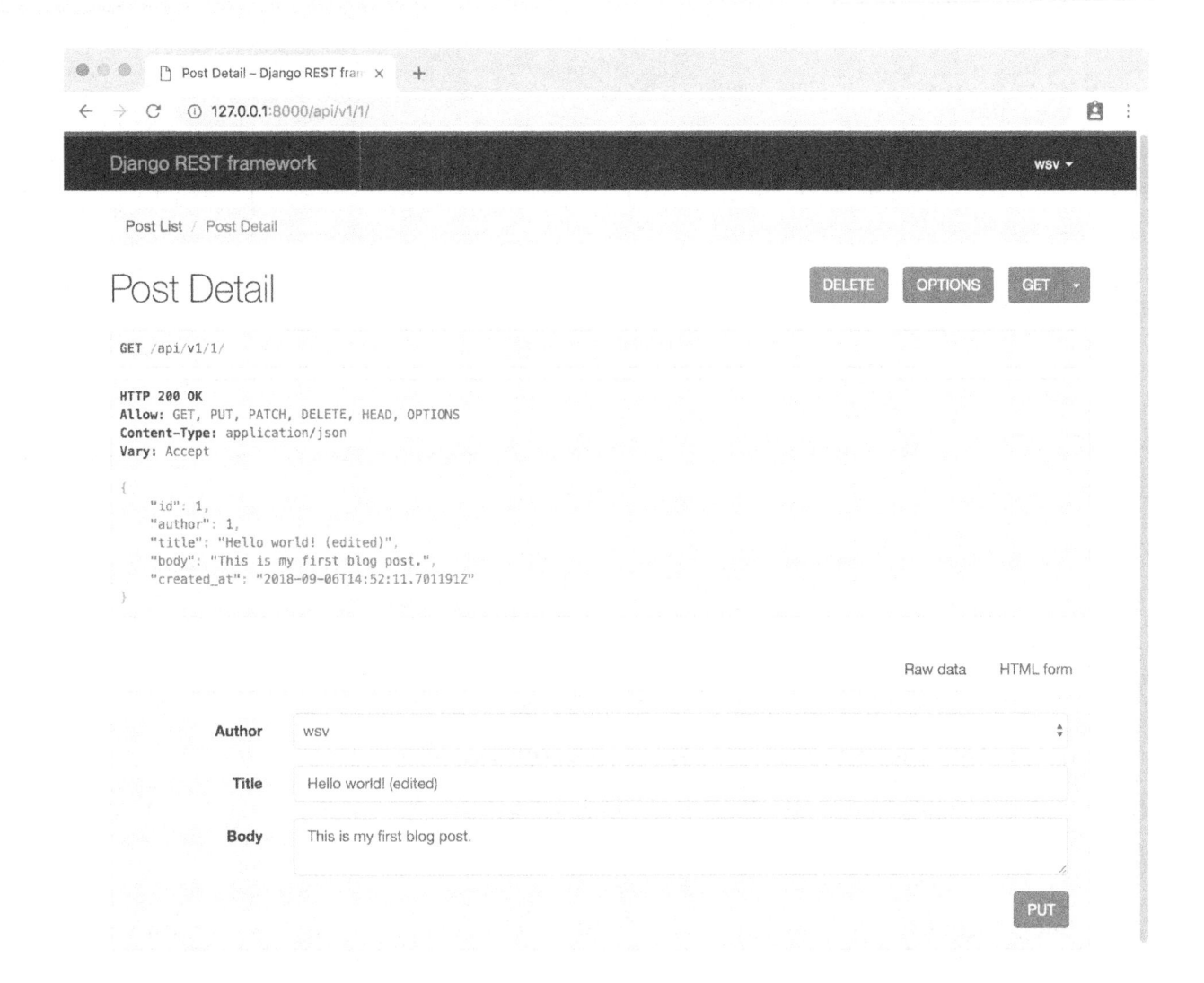

API Detail Superuser

However if you log out and then log in with the `testuser` account the page changes.

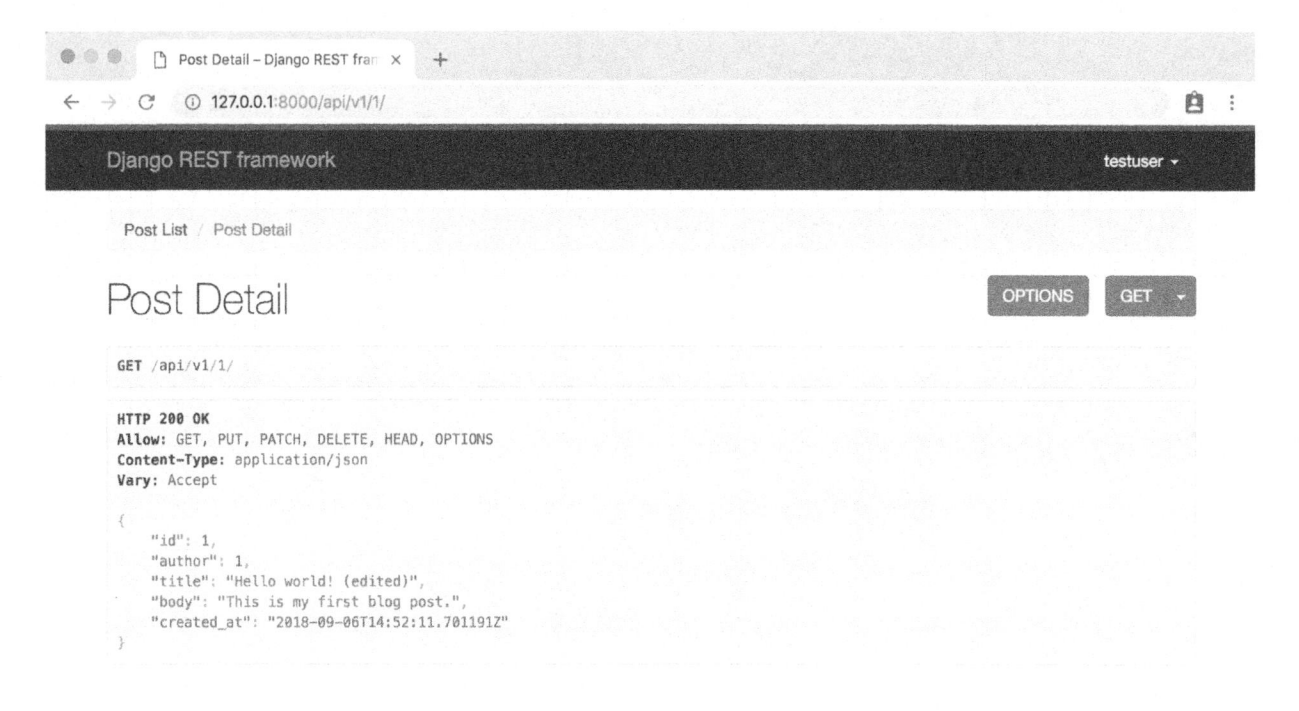

```
┌─────────────────────────────────────────────────────────────┐
│ ● ● ●    [ ] Post Detail – Django REST fram  ×   +          │
│ ← → C   ⓘ 127.0.0.1:8000/api/v1/1/                     📋 ⋮ │
├─────────────────────────────────────────────────────────────┤
│ Django REST framework                              testuser ▾│
├─────────────────────────────────────────────────────────────┤
│ Post List / Post Detail                                     │
│                                                             │
│ Post Detail                            [ OPTIONS ] [ GET ▾ ]│
│                                                             │
│ GET /api/v1/1/                                              │
│                                                             │
│ HTTP 200 OK                                                 │
│ Allow: GET, PUT, PATCH, DELETE, HEAD, OPTIONS               │
│ Content-Type: application/json                              │
│ Vary: Accept                                                │
│                                                             │
│ {                                                           │
│     "id": 1,                                                │
│     "author": 1,                                            │
│     "title": "Hello world! (edited)",                       │
│     "body": "This is my first blog post.",                  │
│     "created_at": "2018-09-06T14:52:11.701191Z"             │
│ }                                                           │
└─────────────────────────────────────────────────────────────┘

**API Detail Testuser**

We **can** view this page since read-only permissions are allowed. However we **can not** make any PUT or DELETE requests due to our custom IsAuthorOrReadOnly permission class.

Note that the generic views will only check the object-level permissions for views that retrieve a single model instance. If you require object-level filtering of list views–for a collection of instances–you'll need to filter by overriding the initial queryset[93].

## Conclusion

Setting proper permissions is a very important part of any API. As a general strategy, it is a good idea to set a strict project-level permissions policy such that only authenticated users can view the API. Then make view-level or custom permissions more accessible as needed on specific API endpoints.

---
[93]http://www.django-rest-framework.org/api-guide/filtering/#overriding-the-initial-queryset
```

Chapter 7: User Authentication

In the previous chapter we updated our APIs permissions, which is also called **authorization**. In this chapter we will implement **authentication** which is the process by which a user can register for a new account, log in with it, and log out.

Within a traditional, monolithic Django website authentication is simpler and involves a session-based cookie pattern which we will review below. But with an API things are a bit trickier. Remember that HTTP is a **stateless protocol** so there is no built-in way to remember if a user is authenticated from one request to the next. Each time a user requests a restricted resource it must verify itself.

The solution is to pass along a unique identifier with each HTTP request. Confusingly there is no universally agreed-upon approach for the form of this identifier and it can take multiple forms. Django REST Framework ships with four different built-in authentication options[94] alone! And there are many more third-party packages that offer additional features like JSON Web Tokens (JWTs).

In this chapter we will thoroughly explore how API authentication works, review the pros and cons of each approach, and then make an informed choice for our *Blog* API. By the end, we will have created API endpoints for sign up, log in, and log out.

Basic Authentication

The most common form of HTTP authentication is known as "Basic" Authentication[95]. When a client makes an HTTP request, it is forced to send an approved authentication

---
[94]http://www.django-rest-framework.org/api-guide/authentication/#sessionauthentication
[95]https://tools.ietf.org/html/rfc7617

credential before access is granted.

The complete request/response flow looks like this:

1. Client makes an HTTP request
2. Server responds with an HTTP response containing a `401 (Unauthorized)` status code and `WWW-Authenticate` HTTP header with details on *how* to authorize
3. Client sends credentials back via the Authorization[96] HTTP header
4. Server checks credentials and responds with either `200 OK` or `403 Forbidden` status code

Once approved, the client sends all future requests with the approved `Authorization` HTTP header credentials.

We can also visualize this exchange as follows:

Diagram

```
Client                                                             Server
------                                                             ------



--------------------------------------->
GET / HTTP/1.1


                                        <---------------------------------------
                                                            HTTP/1.1 401 Unauthorized
                                                            WWW-Authenticate: Basic


--------------------------------------->
GET / HTTP/1.1

Authorization: Basic d3N2OnBhc3N3b3JkMTIz
```

[96]https://developer.mozilla.org/en-US/docs/Web/HTTP/Headers/Authorization

```
                                     <------------------------------------
                                     HTTP/1.1 200 OK
```

Note that the authorization credentials sent are the unencrypted base64 encoded[97] version of `<username>:<password>`. So in my case, this is `wsv:password123` which with base64 encoding is `d3N2OnBhc3N3b3JkMTIz`.

The primary advantage of this approach is its simplicity. But there are several major downsides. First, on *every single request* the server must look up and verify the username and password, which is inefficient. It would be better to do the look up once and then pass a token of some kind that says, this user is approved. Second, user credentials are being passed in clear text–not encrypted at all–over the internet. This is incredibly insecure. Any internet traffic that is not encrypted can easily be captured and reused. Thus basic authentication should **only** be used via HTTPS[98], the secure version of `HTTP`.

Session Authentication

Monolithic websites, like traditional Django, have long used an alternative authentication scheme that is a combination of sessions and cookies. At a high level, the client authenticates with its credentials (username/password) and then receives a *session ID* from the server which is stored as a cookie. This session ID is then passed in the header of every future HTTP request.

When the session ID is passed, the server uses it to look up a session object containing all available information for a given user, including credentials.

---
[97]https://en.wikipedia.org/wiki/Base64
[98]https://en.wikipedia.org/wiki/HTTPS

This approach is **stateful** because a record must be kept and maintained on both the server (the session object) and the client (the session ID).

Let's review the basic flow:

1. A user enters their log in credentials (typically username/password)
2. The server verifies the credentials are correct and generates a session object that is then stored in the database
3. The server sends the client a session ID–not the session object itself–which is stored as a cookie on the browser
4. On all future requests the session ID is included as an HTTP header and, if verified by the database, the request proceeds
5. Once a user logs out of an application, the session ID is destroyed by both the client and server
6. If the user later logs in again, a new session ID is generated and stored as a cookie on the client

The default setting in Django REST Framework is actually a combination of Basic Authentication and Session Authentication. Django's traditional session-based authentication system is used and the session ID is passed in the HTTP header on each request via Basic Authentication.

The advantage of this approach is that it is more secure since user credentials are only sent once, not on every request/response cycle as in Basic Authentication. It is also more efficient since the server does not have to verify the user's credentials each time, it just matches the session ID to the session object which is a fast look up.

There are several downsides however. First, a session ID is only valid within the browser where log in was performed; it will not work across multiple domains. This is an obvious problem when an API needs to support multiple front-ends such as a website and a mobile app. Second, the session object must be kept up-to-date which can be challenging in large sites with multiple servers. How do you maintain the accuracy of a session object across each server? And third, the cookie is sent out for every single request, even those that don't require authentication, which is inefficient.

As a result, it is generally not advised to use a session-based authentication scheme for any API that will have multiple front-ends.

Token Authentication

The third major approach–and the one we will implement in our *Blog* API–is to use token authentication. This is the most popular approach in recent years due to the rise of single page applications.

Token-based authentication is **stateless**: once a client sends the initial user credentials to the server, a unique token is generated and then stored by the client as either a cookie or in local storage[99]. This token is then passed in the header of each incoming HTTP request and the server uses it to verify that a user is authenticated. The server itself does not keep a record of the user, just whether a token is valid or not.

> **Cookies vs localStorage**
>
> Cookies are used for reading **server-side** information. They are smaller (4KB) in size and automatically sent with each HTTP request. LocalStorage is designed for **client-side** information. It is much larger (5120KB) and its contents are not sent by default with each HTTP request. Tokens stored in both cookies and localStorage are vulnerable to XSS attacks. The current best practice is to store tokens in a cookie with the `httpOnly` and `Secure` cookie flags.

Let's look at a simple version of actual HTTP messages in this challenge/response flow. Note that the HTTP header `WWW-Authenticate` specifies the use of a `Token` which

---
[99]https://developer.mozilla.org/en-US/docs/Web/API/Window/localStorage

is used in the response `Authorization` header request.

Diagram

```
Client                                                          Server
------                                                          ------


----------------------------------------->
GET / HTTP/1.1


                                         <------------------------------------
                                                           HTTP/1.1 401 Unauthorized
                                                           WWW-Authenticate: Token


----------------------------------------->
GET / HTTP/1.1
Authorization: Token 401f7ac837da42b97f613d789819ff93537bee6a


                                         <------------------------------------
                                                                    HTTP/1.1 200 OK
```

There are multiple benefits to this approach. Since tokens are stored on the client, scaling the servers to maintain up-to-date session objects is no longer an issue. And tokens can be shared amongst multiple front-ends: the same token can represent a user on the website and the same user on a mobile app. The same session ID can not be shared amongst different front-ends, a major limitation.

A potential downside is that tokens can grow quite large. A token contains all user information, not just an id as with a session id/session object set up. Since the token is sent on every request, managing its size can become a performance issue.

Exactly *how* the token is implemented can also vary substantially. Django REST

Frameworks' built-in TokenAuthentication[100] is deliberately quite basic. As a result, it does not support setting tokens to expire, which is a security improvement that can be added. It also only generates one token per user, so a user on a website and then later a mobile app will use the same token. Since information about the user is stored locally, this can cause problems with maintaining and updating two sets of client information.

JSON Web Tokens (JWTs) are a new, enhanced version of tokens that can be added to Django REST Framework via several third-party packages. JWTs have several benefits including the ability to generate unique client tokens and token expiration. They can either be generated on the server or with a third-party service like Auth0[101]. And JWTs can be encrypted which makes them safer to send over unsecured HTTP connections.

Ultimately the safest bet for most web APIs is to use a token-based authentication scheme. JWTs are a nice, modern addition though they require additional configuration. As a result, in this book we will use the built-in `TokenAuthentication`.

Default Authentication

The first step is to configure our new authentication settings. Django REST Framework comes with a number of settings[102] that are implicitly set. For example, `DEFAULT_PERMISSION_CLASSES` was set to `AllowAny` before we updated it to `IsAuthenticated`.

The `DEFAULT_AUTHENTICATION_CLASSES` are set by default to `SessionAuthentication` and `BasicAuthentication`. Let's explicitly add them to our `blog_project/settings.py` file.

---

[100]http://www.django-rest-framework.org/api-guide/authentication/#tokenauthentication
[101]https://auth0.com/
[102]http://www.django-rest-framework.org/api-guide/settings/

Code

```
REST_FRAMEWORK = {
    'DEFAULT_PERMISSION_CLASSES': [
        'rest_framework.permissions.IsAuthenticated',
    ],
    'DEFAULT_AUTHENTICATION_CLASSES': [ # new
        'rest_framework.authentication.SessionAuthentication',
        'rest_framework.authentication.BasicAuthentication'
    ],
}
```

Why use **both** methods? The answer is they serve different purposes. Sessions are used to power the Browsable API and the ability to log in and log out of it. BasicAuthentication is used to pass the session ID in the HTTP headers for the API itself.

If you revisit the browsable API at http://127.0.0.1:8000/api/v1/[103] it will work just as before. Technically nothing has changed, we've just made the default settings explicit.

Implementing token authentication

Now we need to update our authentication system to use tokens. The first step is to update our DEFAULT_AUTHENTICATION_CLASSES setting to use TokenAuthentication as follows:

---
[103]http://127.0.0.1:8000/api/v1/

Code

```
REST_FRAMEWORK = {
    'DEFAULT_PERMISSION_CLASSES': [
        'rest_framework.permissions.IsAuthenticated',
    ],
    'DEFAULT_AUTHENTICATION_CLASSES': [
        'rest_framework.authentication.SessionAuthentication',
        'rest_framework.authentication.TokenAuthentication', # new
    ],
}
```

We keep `SessionAuthentication` since we still need it for our Browsable API, but now use tokens to pass authentication credentials back and forth in our HTTP headers.

We also need to add the `authtoken` app which generates the tokens on the server. It comes included with Django REST Framework but must be added to our INSTALLED_APPS setting:

Code

```
INSTALLED_APPS = [
    'django.contrib.admin',
    'django.contrib.auth',
    'django.contrib.contenttypes',
    'django.contrib.sessions',
    'django.contrib.messages',
    'django.contrib.staticfiles',

    # 3rd-party apps
    'rest_framework',
    'rest_framework.authtoken', # new
```

```
# Local
'posts.apps.PostsConfig',
]
```

Since we have made changes to our INSTALLED_APPS we need to sync our database. Stop the server with Control+c. Then run the following command.

Command Line

```
(blogapi) $ python manage.py migrate
```

Now start up the server again.

Command Line

```
(blogapi) $ python manage.py runserver
```

If you navigate to the Django admin at http://127.0.0.1:8000/admin/[104] you'll see there is now a Tokens section at the top. Make sure you're logged in with your superuser account to have access.

[104]http://127.0.0.1:8000/admin/

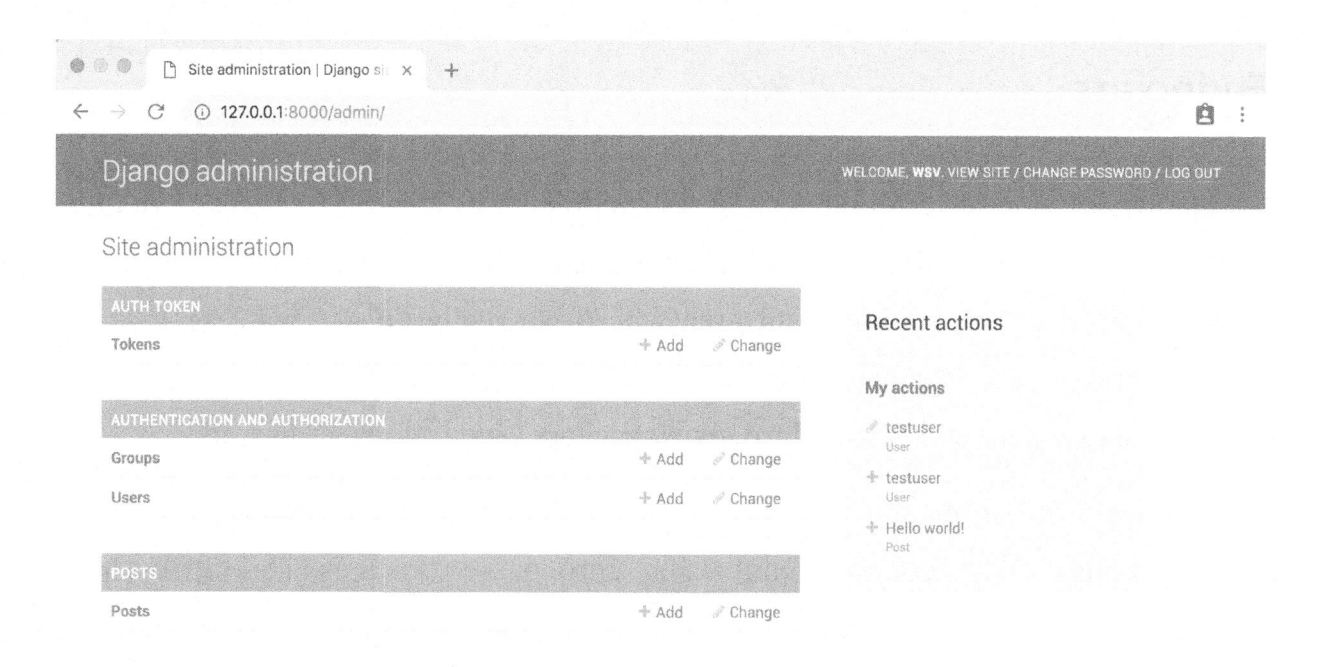

Admin Homepage with Tokens

Click on the link for `Tokens` to go to the Tokens page at:

http://127.0.0.1:8000/admin/authtoken/token/[105].

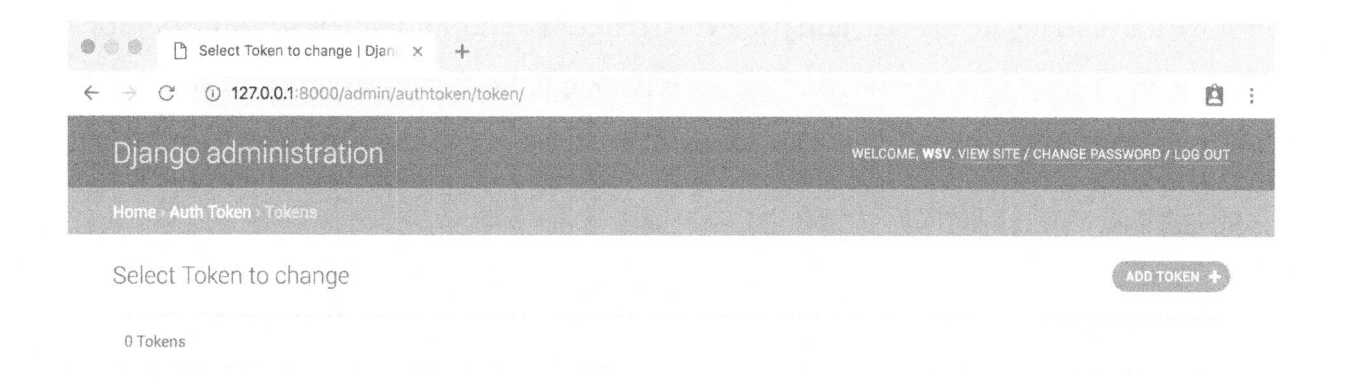

Admin Tokens Page

Currently there are no tokens which might be surprising. After all we have existing users. However the tokens are only generated *after* there is an API call for a user to log in. We have not done that yet so there are no tokens. We will shortly!

---
[105]http://127.0.0.1:8000/admin/authtoken/token/

Endpoints

We also need to create endpoints so users can log in and log out. We *could* create a dedicated `users` app for this purpose and then add our own urls, views, and serializers. However user authentication is an area where we really do not want to make a mistake. And since almost all APIs require this functionality, it makes sense that there are several excellent and tested third-party packages we can use it instead.

Notably we will use django-rest-auth[106] in combination with django-allauth[107] to simplify things. Don't feel bad about using third-party packages. They exist for a reason and even the best Django professionals rely on them all the time. There is no point in reinventing the wheel if you don't have to!

Django-Rest-Auth

First we will add log in, log out, and password reset API endpoints. These come out-of-the-box with the popular `django-rest-auth` package. Stop the server with `Control+c` and then install it.

Command Line

```
(blogapi) $ pipenv install django-rest-auth==0.9.3
```

Add the new app to the `INSTALLED_APPS` config in our `blog_project/settings.py` file.

---

[106]https://github.com/Tivix/django-rest-auth
[107]https://github.com/pennersr/django-allauth

Code

```python
# blog_project/settings.py
INSTALLED_APPS = [
    'django.contrib.admin',
    'django.contrib.auth',
    'django.contrib.contenttypes',
    'django.contrib.sessions',
    'django.contrib.messages',
    'django.contrib.staticfiles',

    # 3rd-party apps
    'rest_framework',
    'rest_framework.authtoken',
    'rest_auth', # new

    # Local
    'posts.apps.PostsConfig',
]
```

Update our `blog_project/urls.py` file with the `rest_auth` package. We're setting the URL routes to `api/v1/rest-auth`.

Code

```
# blog_project/urls.py
from django.contrib import admin
from django.urls import include, path

urlpatterns = [
    path('admin/', admin.site.urls),
    path('api/v1/', include('posts.urls')),
    path('api-auth/', include('rest_framework.urls')),
    path('api/v1/rest-auth/', include('rest_auth.urls')), # new
]
```

And we're done! If you have ever tried to implement your own user authentication endpoints, it is truly amazing how much time–and headache–`django-rest-auth` saves for us.

Now we can spin up the server to see what `django-rest-auth` has provided.

Command Line

```
(blogapi) $ python manage.py runserver
```

We have a working log in endpoint at http://127.0.0.1:8000/api/v1/rest-auth/login/[108].

[108] http://127.0.0.1:8000/api/v1/rest-auth/login/

API Log In Endpoint

And a log out endpoint at http://127.0.0.1:8000/api/v1/rest-auth/logout/[109].

---
[109]http://127.0.0.1:8000/api/v1/rest-auth/logout/

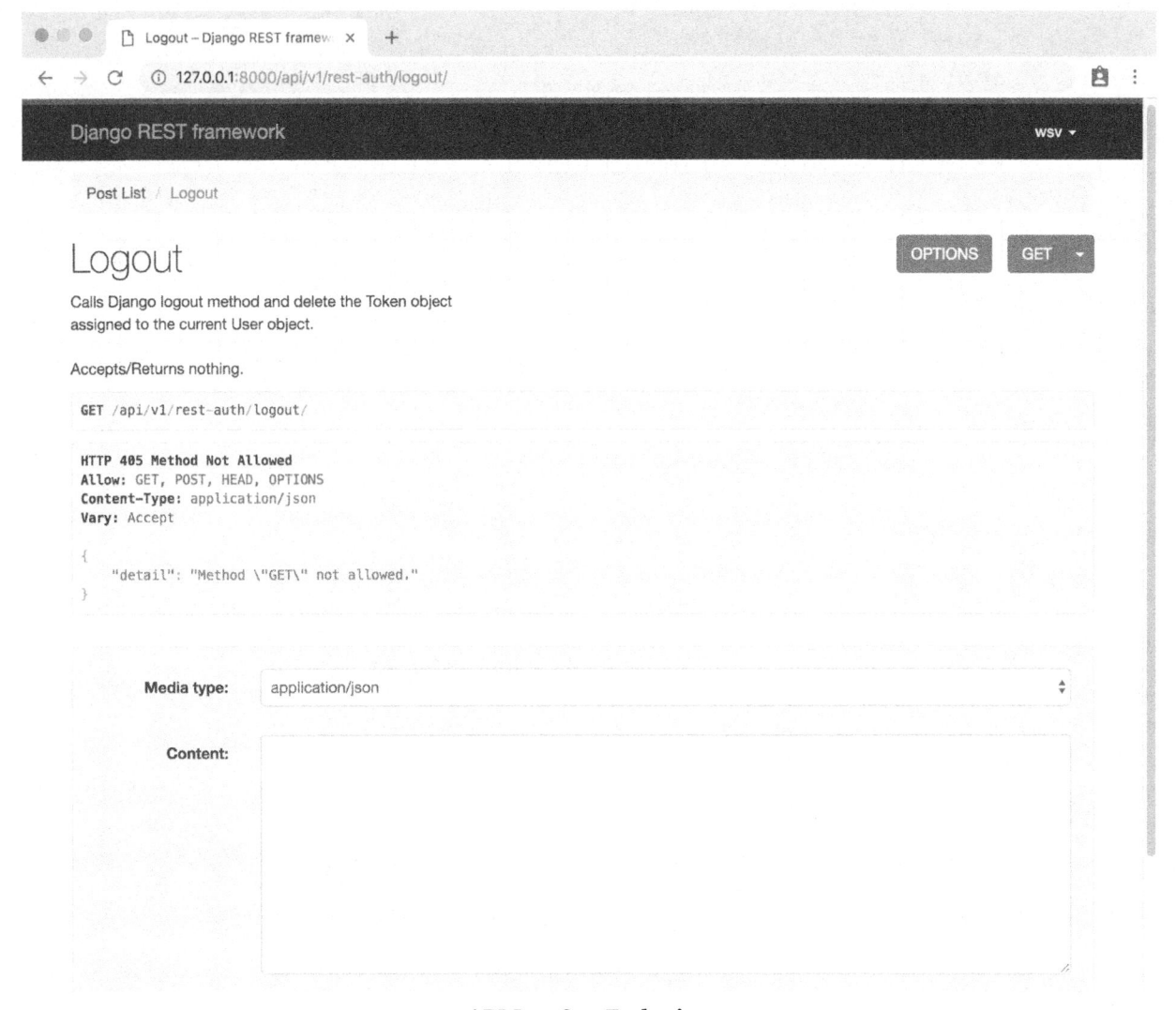

API Log Out Endpoint

There are also endpoints for password reset:

http://127.0.0.1:8000/api/v1/rest-auth/password/reset[110]

---
[110]http://127.0.0.1:8000/api/v1/rest-auth/password/reset

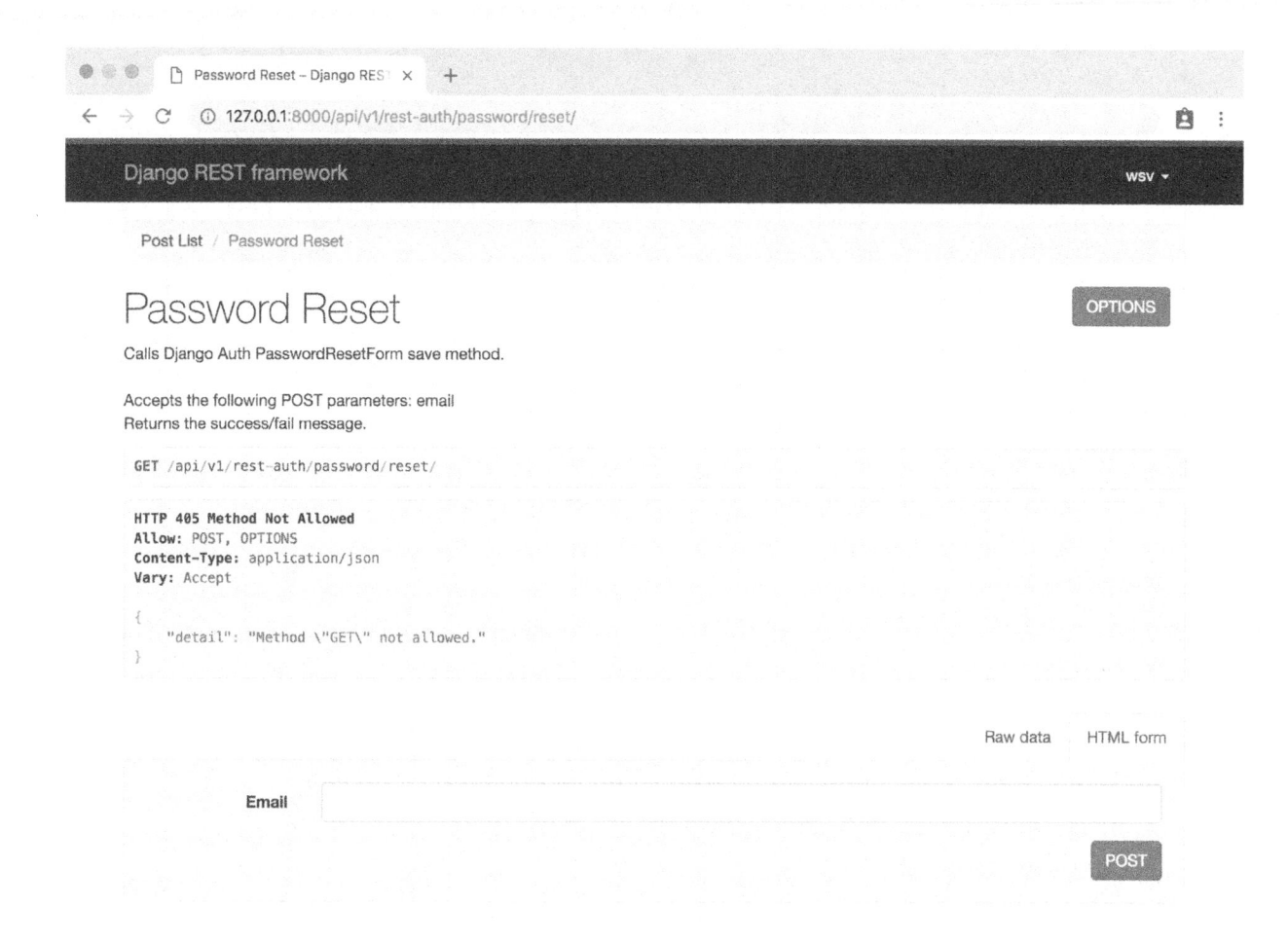

API Password Reset

And for password reset confirmed:

http://127.0.0.1:8000/api/v1/rest-auth/password/reset/confirm[111]

---
[111]http://127.0.0.1:8000/api/v1/rest-auth/password/reset/confirm

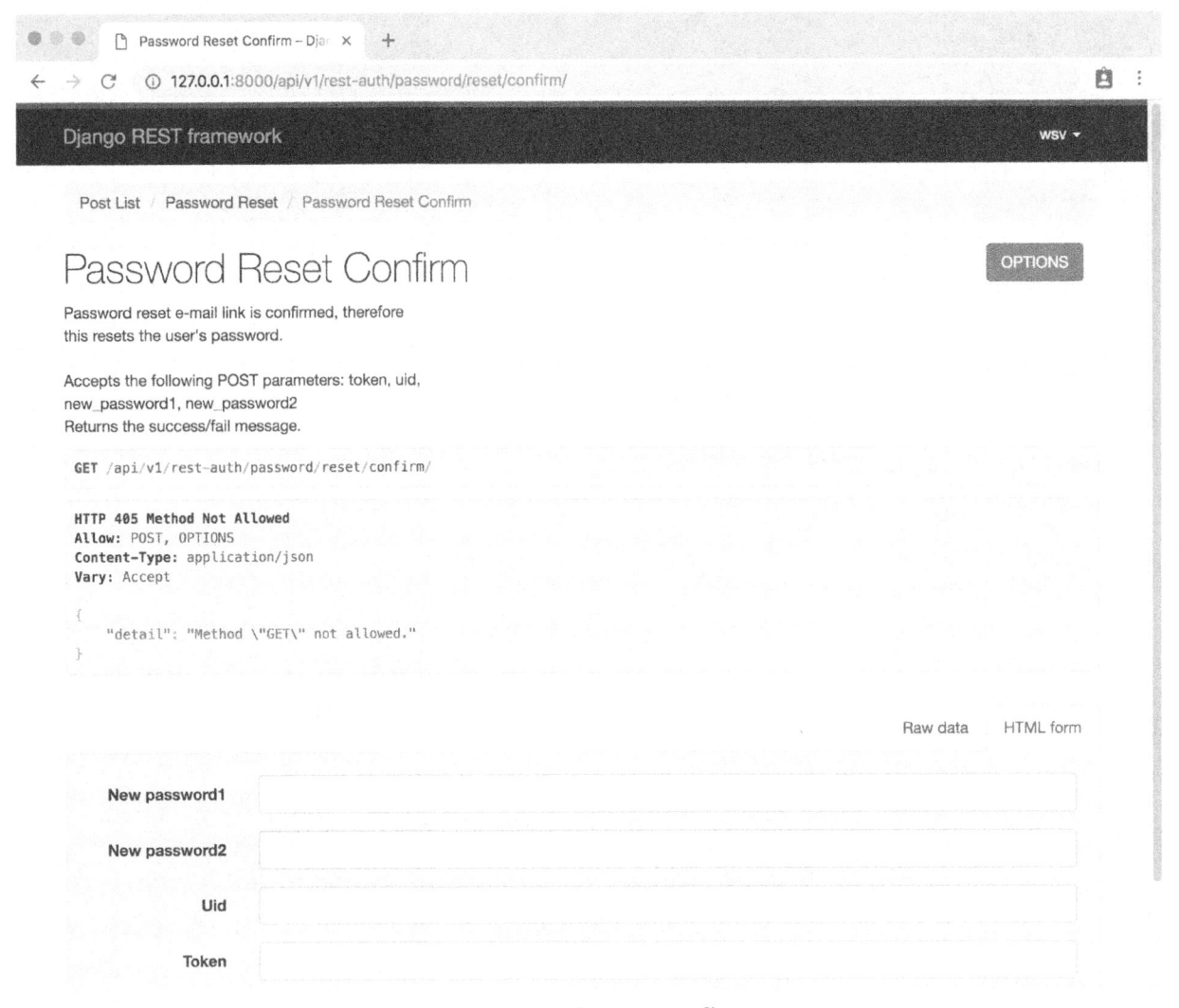

API Password Reset Confirm

User Registration

Next up is our user registration, or sign up, endpoint. Traditional Django does not ship with built-in views or URLs for user registration and neither does Django REST Framework. Which means we need to write our own code from scratch; a somewhat risky approach given the seriousness–and security implications–of getting this wrong.

A popular approach is to use the third-party package django-allauth[112] which comes with user registration as well as a number of additional features to the Django auth system such as social authentication via Facebook, Google, Twitter, etc. If we add `rest_auth.registration` from the `django-rest-auth` package then we have user registration endpoints too!

Stop the local server with `Control+c` and install `django-allauth`.

Command Line

```
(blogapi) $ pipenv install django-allauth==0.37.1
```

Then update our `INSTALLED_APPS` setting. We must add several new configs:

- `django.contrib.sites`
- `allauth`
- `allauth.account`
- `allauth.socialaccount`
- `rest_auth.registration`

Make sure to also include `EMAIL_BACKEND` and `SITE_ID`. Technically it does not matter where in the `settings.py` file they are placed, but it's common to add additional configs like that at the bottom.

---

[112]https://github.com/pennersr/django-allauth

Code

```python
# blog_project/settings.py
INSTALLED_APPS = [
    'django.contrib.admin',
    'django.contrib.auth',
    'django.contrib.contenttypes',
    'django.contrib.sessions',
    'django.contrib.messages',
    'django.contrib.staticfiles',
    'django.contrib.sites', # new

    # 3rd-party apps
    'rest_framework',
    'rest_framework.authtoken',
    'allauth', # new
    'allauth.account', # new
    'allauth.socialaccount', # new
    'rest_auth',
    'rest_auth.registration', # new

    # Local
    'posts.apps.PostsConfig',
]

...


EMAIL_BACKEND = 'django.core.mail.backends.console.EmailBackend' # new

SITE_ID = 1 # new
```

The email back-end config is needed since by default an email will be sent when a new user is registered, asking them to confirm their account. Rather than *also* set up an email server, we will output the emails to the console with the `console.EmailBackend` setting.

`SITE_ID` is part of the built-in Django "sites" framework[113] which is a way to host multiple websites from the same Django project. We obviously only have one site we are working on here but `django-allauth` uses the sites framework, so we must specify a default setting.

Ok. We've added new apps so it's time to update the database.

Command Line

```
(blogapi) $ python manage.py migrate
```

Then add a new URL route for registration.

Code

```
# blog_project/urls.py
from django.contrib import admin
from django.urls import include, path


urlpatterns = [
    path('admin/', admin.site.urls),
    path('api/v1/', include('posts.urls')),
    path('api-auth/', include('rest_framework.urls')),
    path('api/v1/rest-auth/', include('rest_auth.urls')),
    path('api/v1/rest-auth/registration/', # new
```

---
[113] https://docs.djangoproject.com/en/2.1/ref/contrib/sites/

```
        include('rest_auth.registration.urls')),
]
```

And we're done. We can run the local server.

Command Line

```
(blogapi) $ python manage.py runserver
```

There is now a user registration endpoint at:

http://127.0.0.1:8000/api/v1/rest-auth/registration/[114]

---

[114] http://127.0.0.1:8000/api/v1/rest-auth/registration/

API Register

Tokens

To make sure everything works, create a third user account via the browsable API endpoint. I've called my user `testuser2`. Then click on the "POST" button.

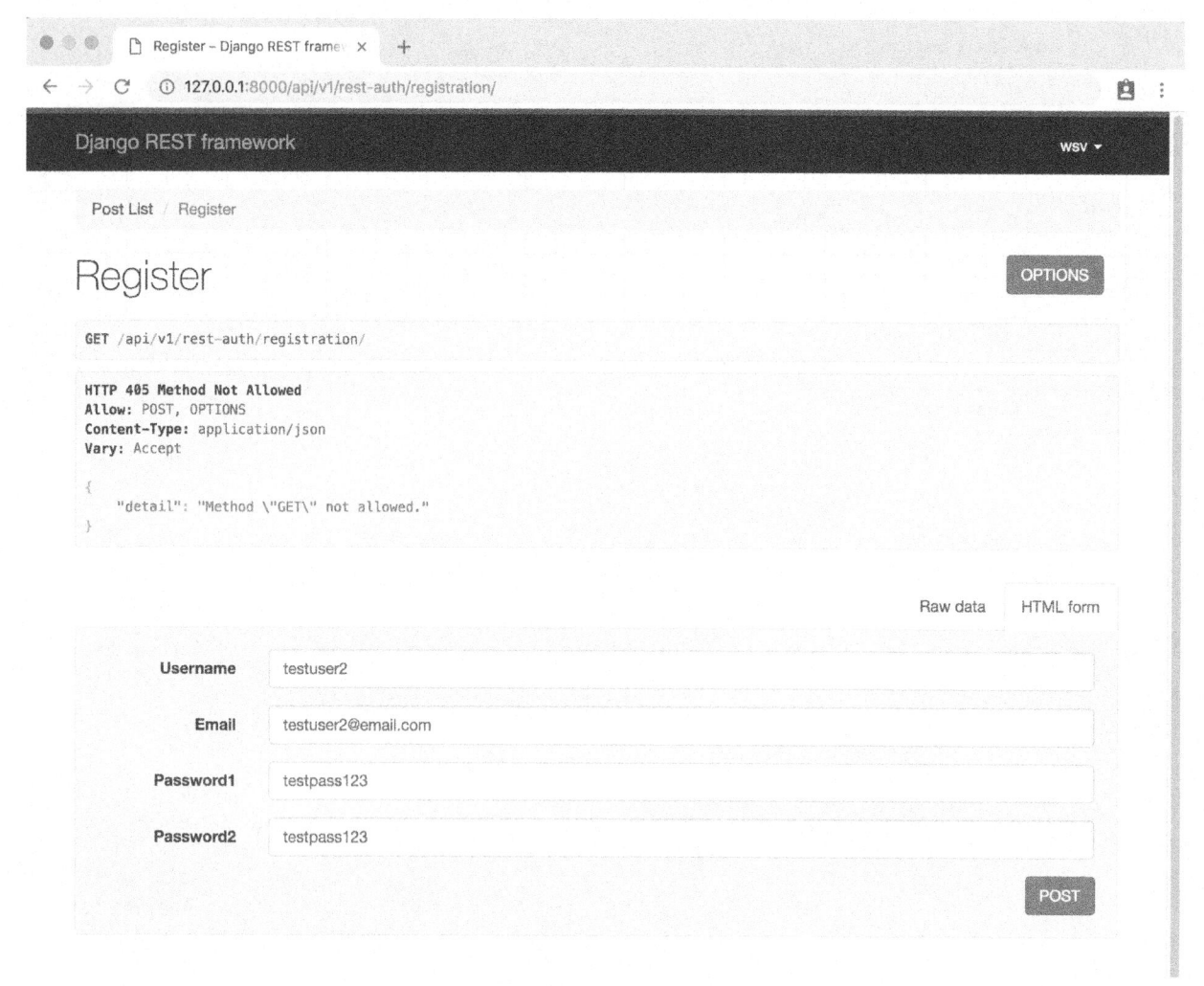

API Register New User

The next screen shows the HTTP response from the server. Our user registration `POST` was successful, hence the status code `HTTP 201 Created` at the top. The return value `key` is the auth token for this new user.

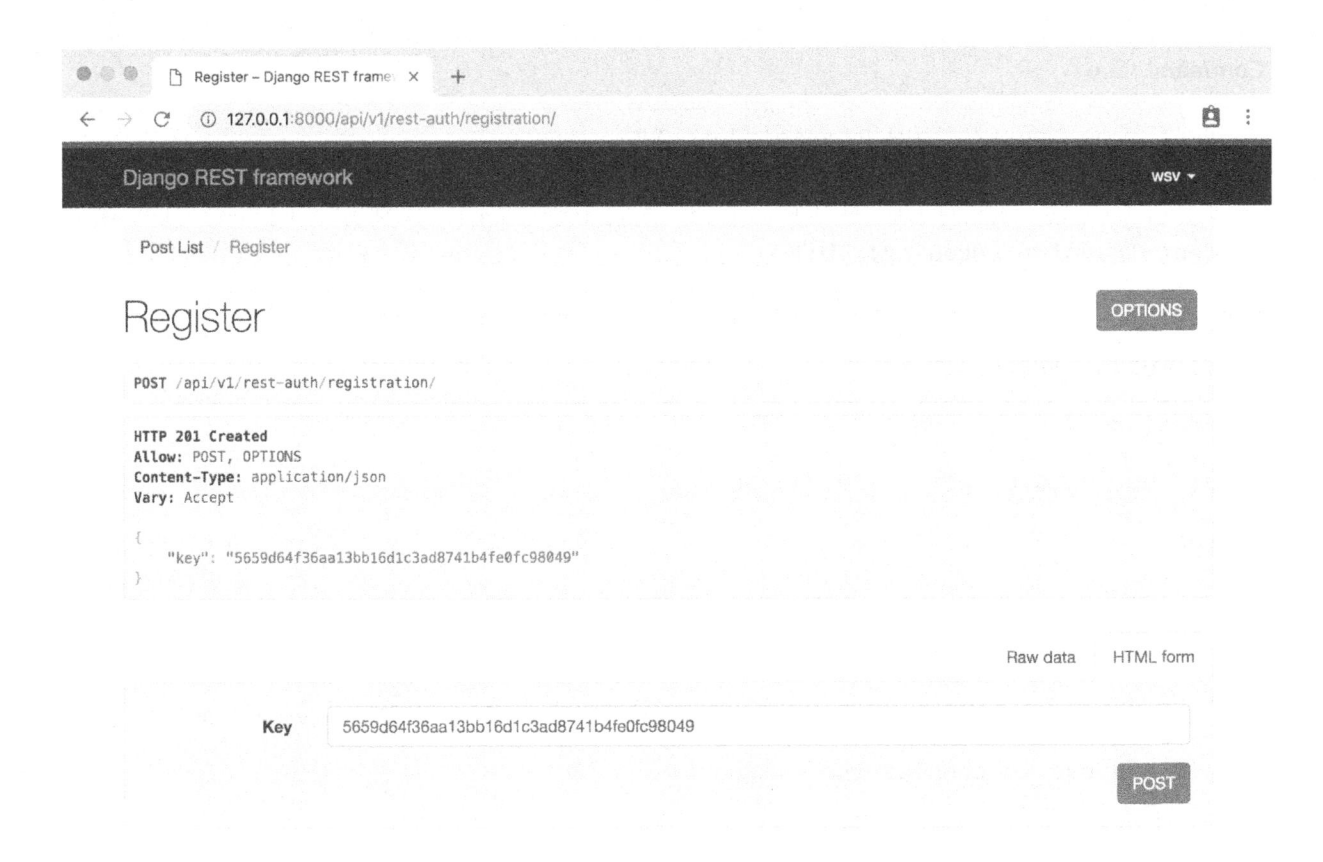

API Auth Key

If you look at the command line console, an email has been automatically generated by `django-allauth`. This default text can be updated and an email SMTP server added with additional configuration that is covered in *Django for Beginners*.

Command Line

```
Content-Type: text/plain; charset="utf-8"
MIME-Version: 1.0
Content-Transfer-Encoding: 7bit
Subject: [example.com] Please Confirm Your E-mail Address
From: webmaster@localhost
To: testuser2@email.com
Date: Thu, 06 Sep 2018 19:29:24 -0000
Message-ID: <153626216499.84718.7765647716299907673@1.0.0.127.in-addr.arpa>


Hello from example.com!
You're receiving this e-mail because user testuser2 has given yours as an\
e-mail address to connect their account.


To confirm this is correct, go to http://127.0.0.1:8000/api/v1/rest-auth/\
registration/account-confirm-email/MQ:1fxzy0:4y-f6DqQFZVNB_-PgBI4Iq_M4iM/


Thank you from example.com!
example.com
```

Switch over to the Django admin in your web browser at http://127.0.0.1:8000/admin/[115]. You will need to use your superuser account for this.

Then click on the link for Tokens at the top of the page.

---
[115]http://127.0.0.1:8000/admin/

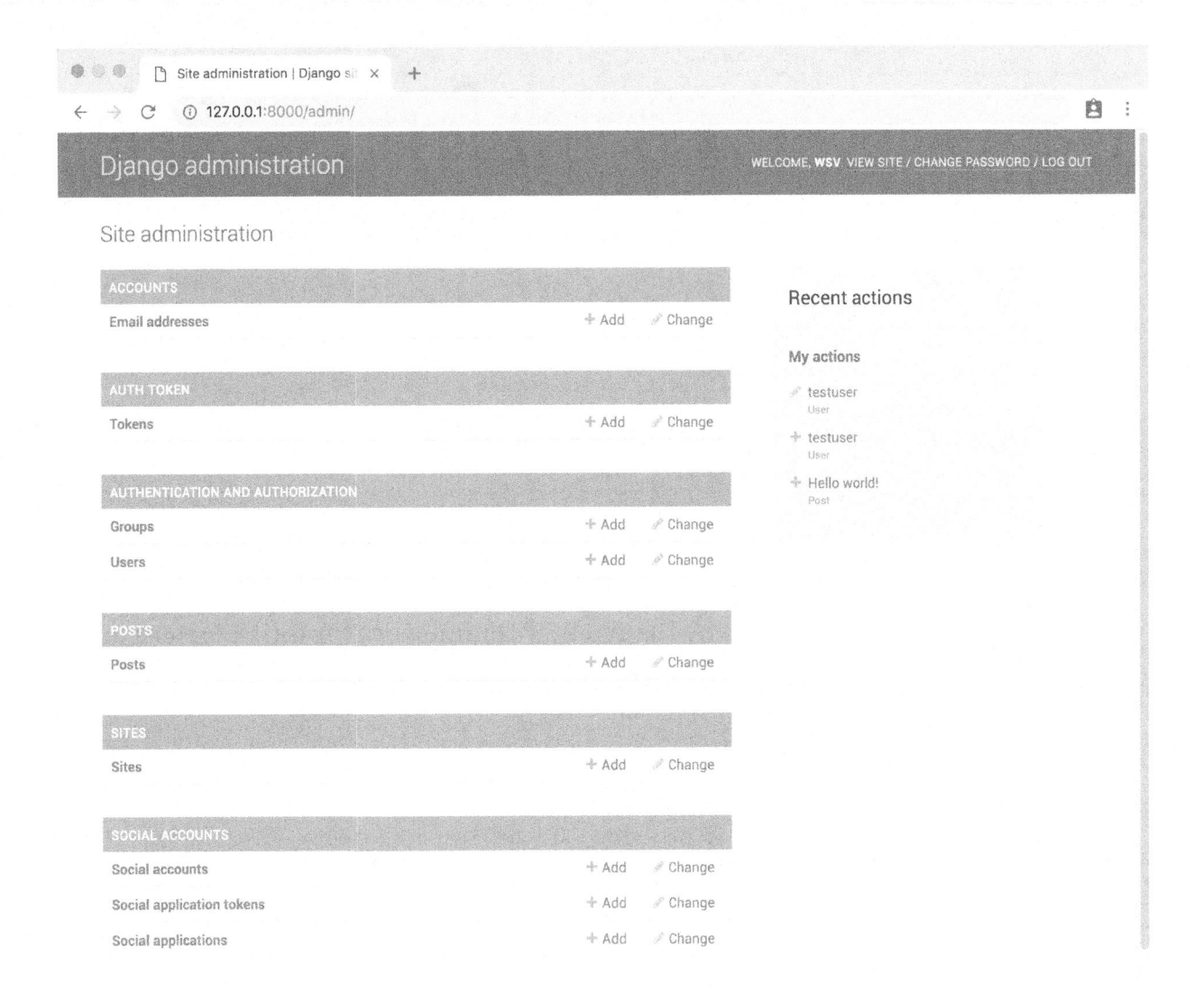

Admin Home with Tokens

You will be redirected to the tokens page which is located at:

http://127.0.0.1:8000/admin/authtoken/token/[116].

---
[116]http://127.0.0.1:8000/admin/authtoken/token/

![Django admin tokens screenshot]

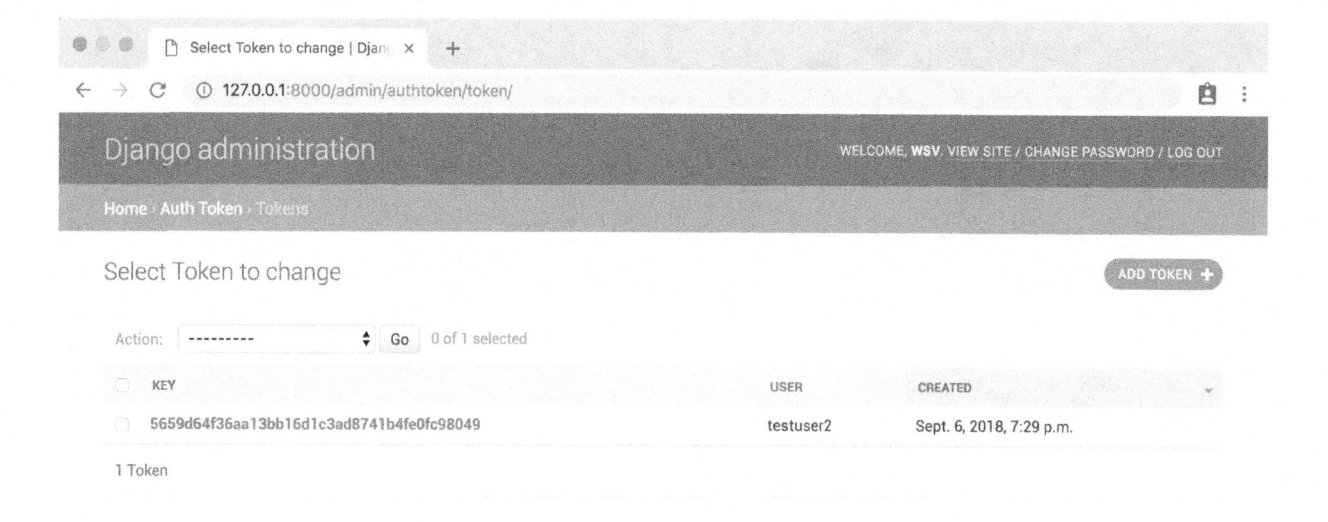

Admin Tokens

A single token has been generated by Django REST Framework for the `testuser2` user. As additional users are created via the API, their tokens will appear here, too.

A logical question is, Why are there are no tokens for our superuser account or `testuser`? The answer is that we created those accounts before token authentication was added. But no worries, once we log in with either account via the API a token will automatically be added and available.

Moving on, let's log in with our new `testuser2` account. Open your web browser to http://127.0.0.1:8000/api/v1/rest-auth/login/[117].

Enter the information for our `testuser2` account. Click on the "POST" button.

---
[117]http://127.0.0.1:8000/api/v1/rest-auth/login/

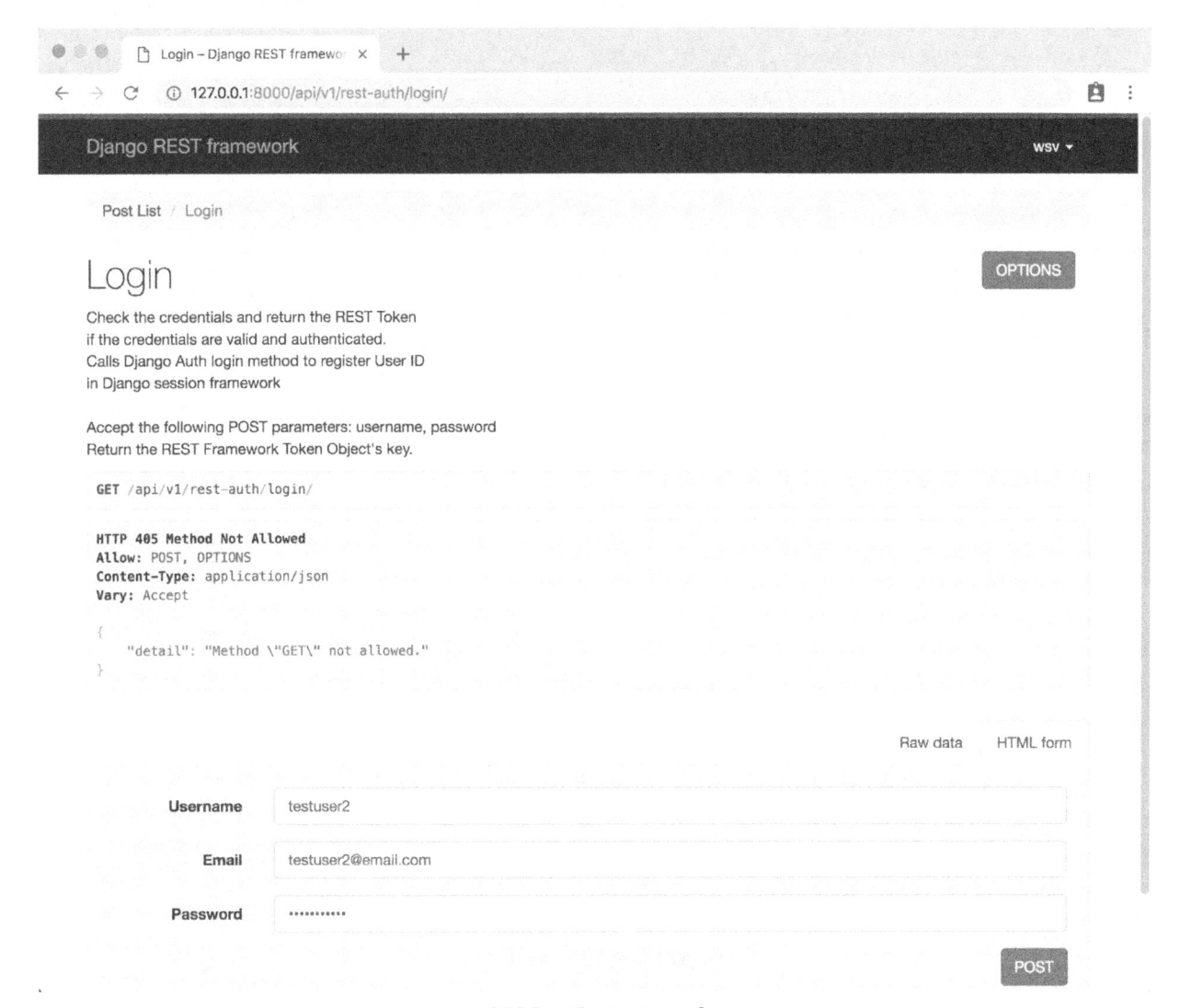

API Log In testuser2

Two things have happened. In the upper righthand corner, our user account `testuser2` is visible, confirming that we are now logged in. Also the server has sent back an HTTP response with the token.

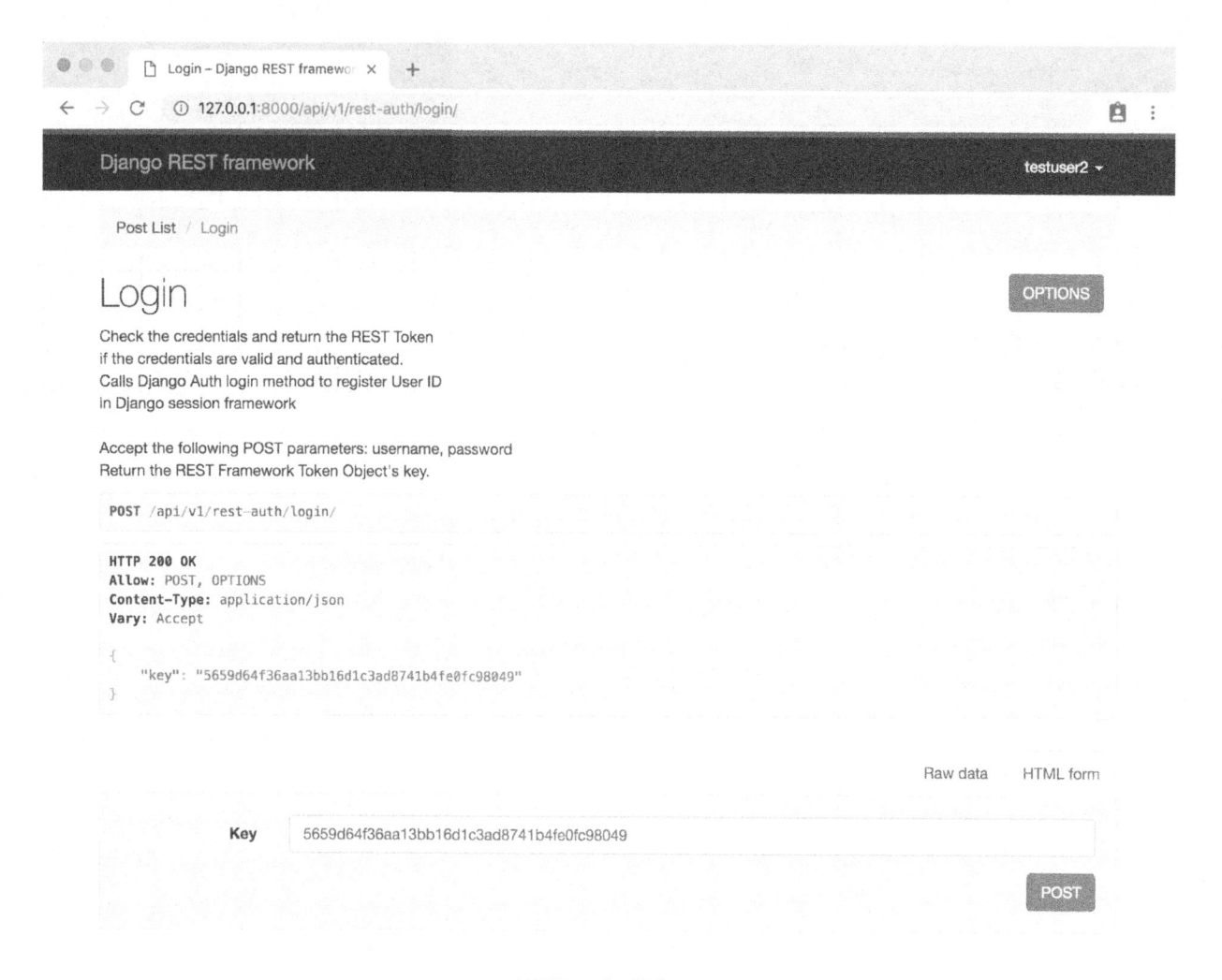

API Log In Token

In our front-end framework, we would need to capture and store this token on the client either in localStorage[118] or as a cookie. Then configure our application so that all future requests include the token in the header as a way to authenticate the user.

Conclusion

User authentication is one of the hardest areas to grasp when first working with web APIs. Without the benefit of a monolithic structure, we as developers have to deeply understand and configure our HTTP request/response cycles appropriately.

---
[118]https://developer.mozilla.org/en-US/docs/Web/API/Window/localStorage

Django REST Framework comes with a lot of built-in support for this process, including built-in `TokenAuthentication`. However developers must configure additional areas like user registration and dedicated urls/views themselves. As a result, a popular, powerful, and secure approach is to rely on the third-party packages `django-rest-auth` and `django-allauth` to minimize the amount of code we have to write from scratch.

Chapter 8: Viewsets and Routers

Viewsets[119] and routers[120] are tools within Django REST Framework that can speed-up API development. They are an additional layer of abstraction on top of views and URLs. The primary benefit is that a single viewset can replace multiple related views. And a router can automatically generate URLs for the developer. In larger projects with many endpoints this means a developer has to write less code. It is also, arguably, easier for an experienced developer to understand and reason about a small number of viewset and router combinations than a long list of individual views and URLs.

In this chapter we will add two new API endpoints to our existing project and see how switching from views and URLs to viewsets and routers can achieve the same functionality with far less code.

User endpoints

Currently we have the following API endpoints in our project. They are all prefixed with `api/v1/` which is not shown for brevity:

---

[119] http://www.django-rest-framework.org/api-guide/viewsets/
[120] http://www.django-rest-framework.org/api-guide/routers/

Diagram

```
|Endpoint                          |HTTP Verb|
|----------------------------------|---------|
|/                                 |GET      |
|/:pk/                             |GET      |
|/rest-auth/registration           |POST     |
|/rest-auth/login                  |POST     |
|/rest-auth/logout                 |GET      |
|/rest-auth/password/reset         |POST     |
|/rest-auth/password/reset/confirm |POST     |
```

The first two endpoints were created by us while `django-rest-auth` provided the five others. Let's now add two additional endpoints to list all users and individual users. This is a common feature in many APIs and it will make it clearer why refactoring our views and URLs to viewsets and routers can make sense.

Traditional Django has a built-in `User` model class that we have already used in the previous chapter for authentication. So we do not need to create a new database model. Instead we just need to wire up new endpoints. This process *always* involves the following three steps:

- new serializer class for the model
- new views for each endpoint
- new URL routes for each endpoint

Start with our serializer. We need to import the `User` model and then create a `UserSerializer` class that uses it. Then add it to our existing `posts/serializers.py` file.

Code

```python
# posts/serializers.py
from django.contrib.auth import get_user_model # new
from rest_framework import serializers

from .models import Post


class PostSerializer(serializers.ModelSerializer):

    class Meta:
        model = Post
        fields = ('id', 'author', 'title', 'body', 'created_at',)


class UserSerializer(serializers.ModelSerializer): # new

    class Meta:
        model = get_user_model()
        fields = ('id', 'username',)
```

It's worth noting that while we have used `get_user_model` to reference the `User` model here, there are actually three different ways to reference[121] the `User` model in Django.

By using `get_user_model` we ensure that we are referring to the correct user model, whether it is the default `User` or a custom user model[122] as is often defined in new Django projects.

Moving on we need to define views for *each* endpoint. First add `UserSerializer` to the list of imports. Then create both a `UserList` class that lists out all users and a

---
[121]https://docs.djangoproject.com/en/2.1/topics/auth/customizing/#referencing-the-user-model
[122]https://docs.djangoproject.com/en/2.1/topics/auth/customizing/#specifying-a-custom-user-model

`UserDetail` class that provides a detail view of an individual user. Just as with our `post` views we can use `ListCreateAPIView` and `RetrieveUpdateDestroyAPIView` here.

For each we only want read-only or `GET` functionality. This means we can use `ListAPIView` and `RetrieveUpdateDestroyAPIView`. We also need to reference the users model via `get_user_model` so it is imported on the top line.

Code

```python
# posts/views.py
from django.contrib.auth import get_user_model # new
from rest_framework import generics

from .models import Post
from .permissions import IsAuthorOrReadOnly
from .serializers import PostSerializer, UserSerializer # new


class PostList(generics.ListCreateAPIView):
    queryset = Post.objects.all()
    serializer_class = PostSerializer


class PostDetail(generics.RetrieveUpdateDestroyAPIView):
    permission_classes = (IsAuthorOrReadOnly,)
    queryset = Post.objects.all()
    serializer_class = PostSerializer


class UserList(generics.ListCreateAPIView): # new
    queryset = get_user_model().objects.all()
```

```
    serializer_class = UserSerializer


class UserDetail(generics.RetrieveUpdateDestroyAPIView): # new
    queryset = get_user_model().objects.all()
    serializer_class = UserSerializer
```

If you notice, there is quite a bit of repetition here. Both `Post` views and `User` views have the *exact same* `queryset` and `serializer_class`. Maybe those could be combined in some way to save code?

Finally we have our URL routes. Make sure to import our new `UserList`, and `UserDetail` views. Then we can use the prefix `users/` for each.

Code

```
# posts/urls.py
from django.urls import path

from .views import UserList, UserDetail, PostList, PostDetail # new

urlpatterns = [
    path('users/', UserList.as_view()), # new
    path('users/<int:pk>/', UserDetail.as_view()), # new
    path('', PostList.as_view()),
    path('<int:pk>/', PostDetail.as_view()),
]
```

And we're done. Make sure the local server is still running and jump over to the browsable API to confirm everything works as expected.

Our user list endpoint is located at http://127.0.0.1:8000/api/v1/users/[123]

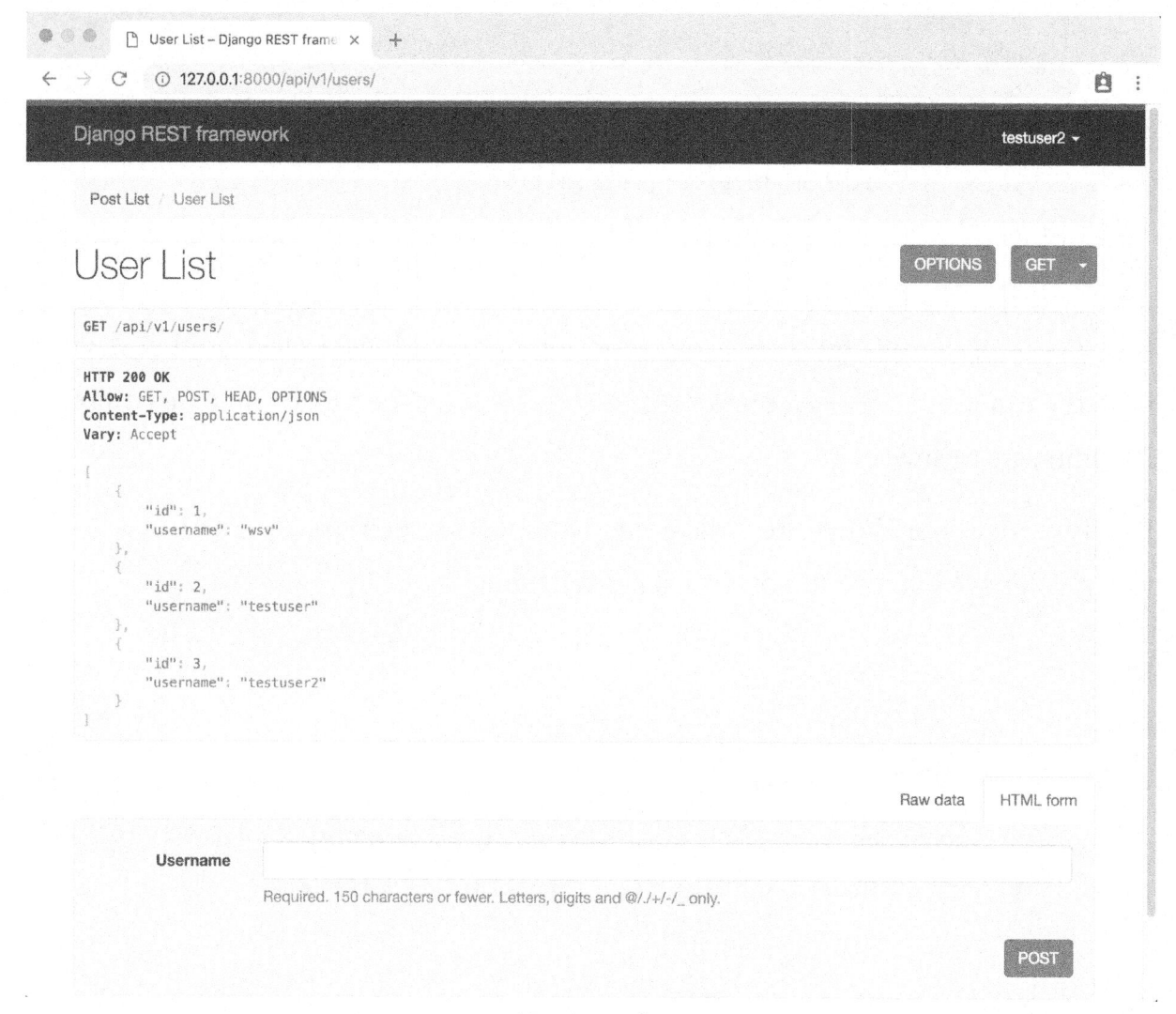

API Users List

The status code is `200 OK` which means everything is working. We can see our three existing users.

A user detail endpoint is available at the primary key for each user. So our superuser account is located at: http://127.0.0.1:8000/api/v1/users/1/[124].

---

[123]http://127.0.0.1:8000/api/v1/users/
[124]http://127.0.0.1:8000/api/v1/users/1/

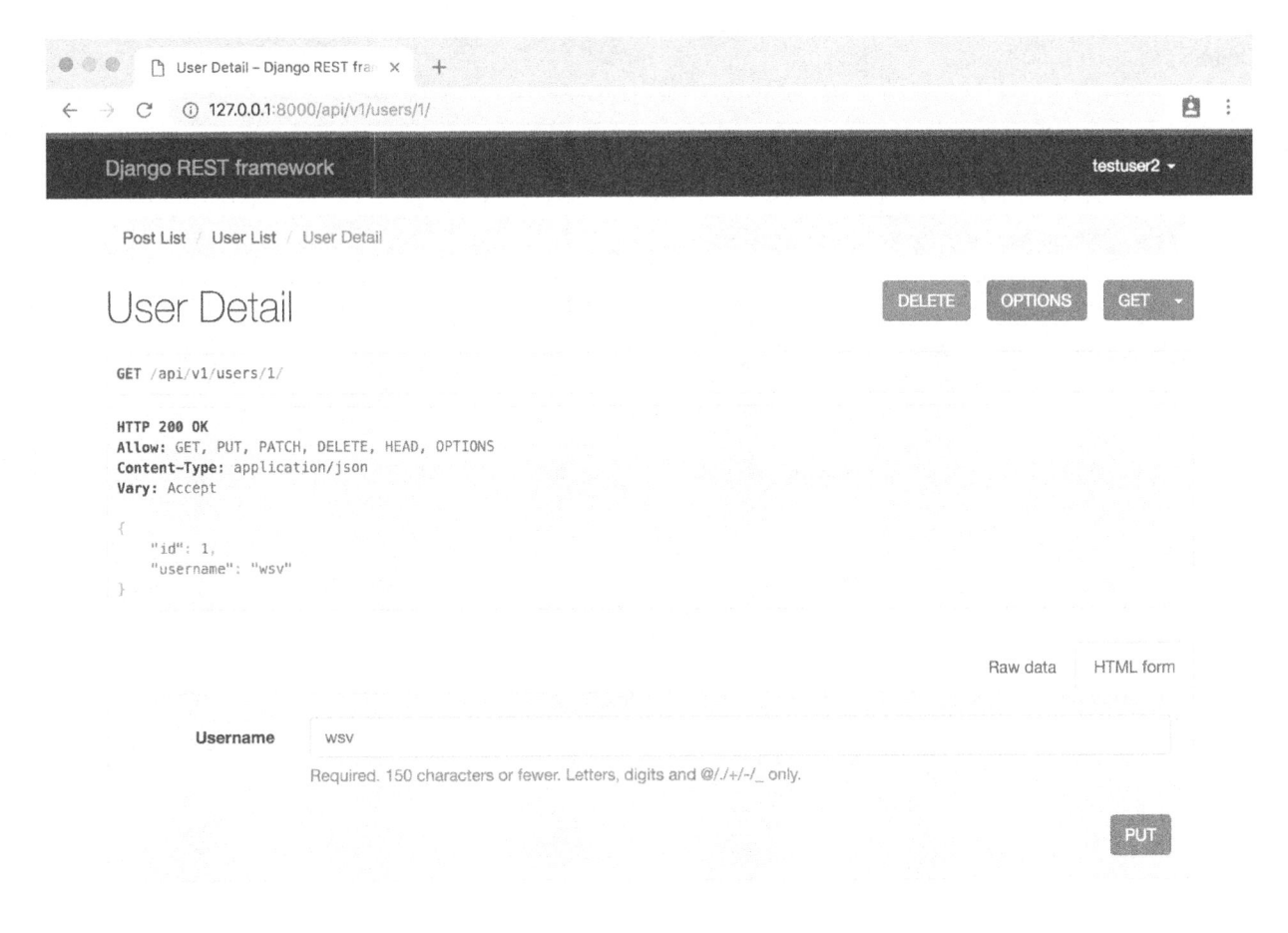

API User Instance

Viewsets

A viewset is a way to combine the logic for multiple related views into a single class. In other words, one viewset can replace multiple views. Currently we have four views: two for blog posts and two for users. We can instead mimic the same functionality with two viewsets: one for blog posts and one for users.

The tradeoff is that there is a loss in readability for fellow developers who are *not* intimately familiar with viewsets. So it's a trade-off.

Here is what the code looks like in our updated `posts/views.py` file when we swap in viewsets.

Code

```python
# posts/views.py
from django.contrib.auth import get_user_model
from rest_framework import viewsets # new

from .models import Post
from .permissions import IsAuthorOrReadOnly
from .serializers import PostSerializer, UserSerializer


class PostViewSet(viewsets.ModelViewSet): # new
    permission_classes = (IsAuthorOrReadOnly,)
    queryset = Post.objects.all()
    serializer_class = PostSerializer


class UserViewSet(viewsets.ModelViewSet): # new
    queryset = get_user_model().objects.all()
    serializer_class = UserSerializer
```

At the top instead of importing `generics` from `rest_framework` we are now importing `viewsets` on the second line. Then we are using ModelViewSet[125] which provides both a list view and a detail view for us. And we no longer have to repeat the same `queryset` and `serializer_class` for each view as we did previously!

[125]http://www.django-rest-framework.org/api-guide/viewsets/#modelviewset

Routers

Routers[126] work directly with viewsets to automatically generate URL patterns for us. Our current `posts/urls.py` file has four URL patterns: two for blog posts and two for users. We can instead adopt a single route for each viewset. So two routes instead of four URL patterns. That sounds better, right?

Django REST Framework has two default routers: SimpleRouter[127] and DefaultRouter[128]. We will use `SimpleRouter` but it's also possible to create custom routers for more advanced functionality.

Here is what the updated code looks like:

Code

```python
# posts/urls.py
from django.urls import path
from rest_framework.routers import SimpleRouter

from .views import UserViewSet, PostViewSet

router = SimpleRouter()
router.register('users', UserViewSet, base_name='users')
router.register('', PostViewSet, base_name='posts')

urlpatterns = router.urls
```

On the top line `SimpleRouter` is imported, along with our views. The `router` is set to `SimpleRouter` and we "register" each viewset for `Users` and `Posts`. Finally we set our

---

[126] http://www.django-rest-framework.org/api-guide/routers/
[127] http://www.django-rest-framework.org/api-guide/routers/#simplerouter
[128] http://www.django-rest-framework.org/api-guide/routers/#defaultrouter

URLs to use the new router.

Go ahead and check out our four endpoints now!

The User List is the same.

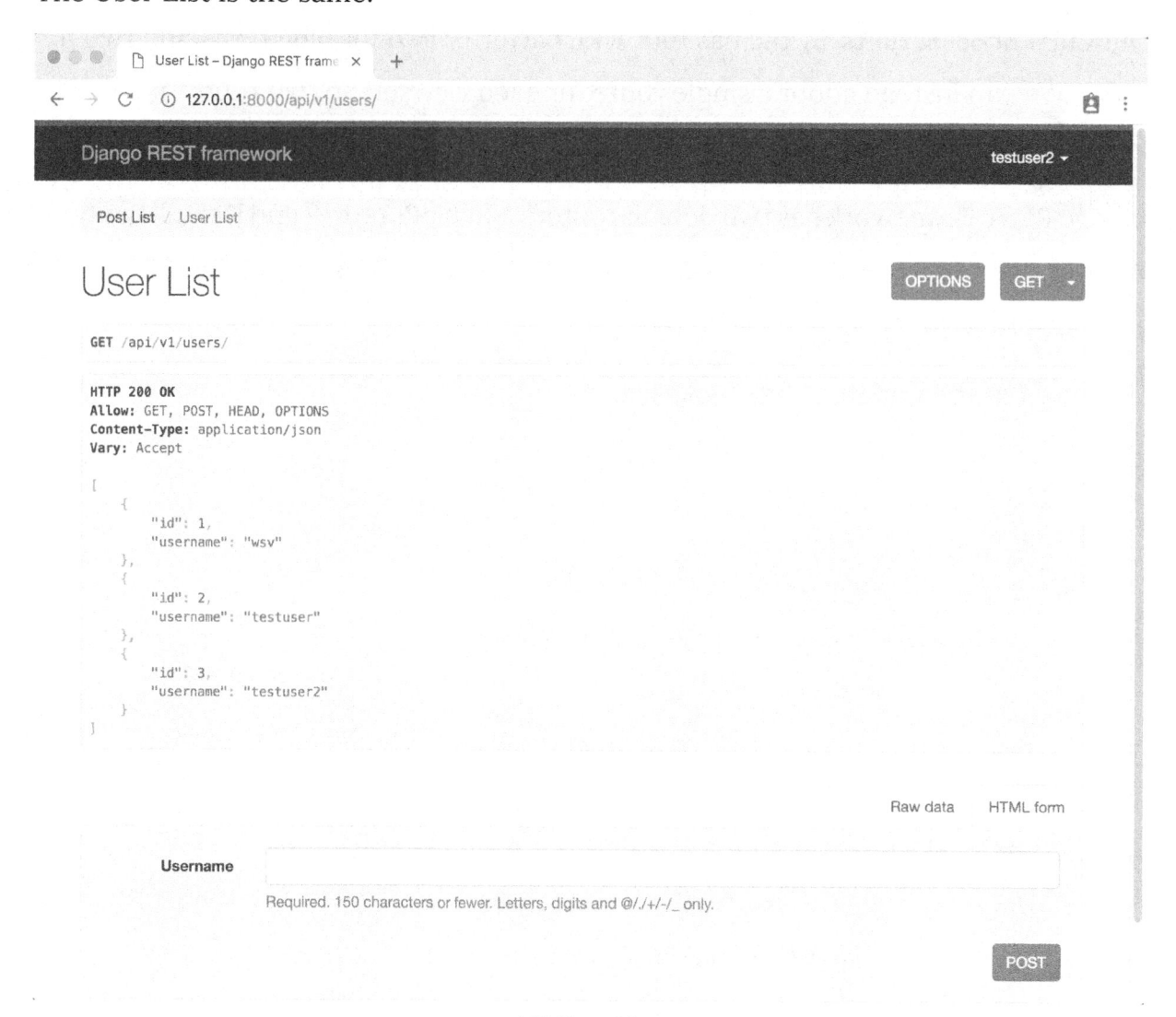

API User List

However the detail view is a little different. It is now called "User Instance" instead of "User Detail" and there is an additional "delete" option which is built-in to ModelViewSet[129].

---
[129]http://www.django-rest-framework.org/api-guide/viewsets/#modelviewset

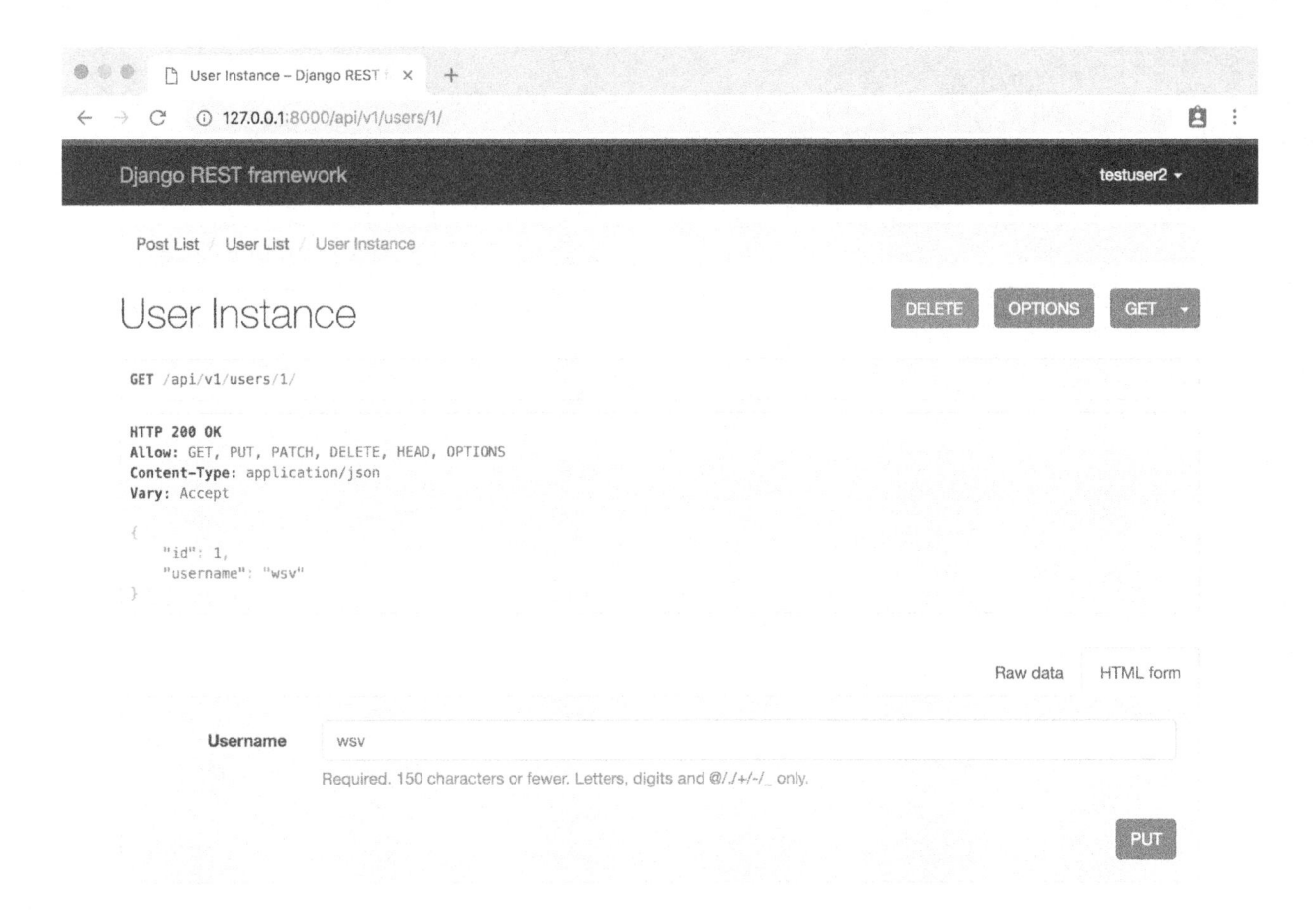

API User Detail

It is possible to customize viewsets but an important tradeoff in exchange for writing a bit less code with viewsets is the default settings may require some additional configuration to match exactly what you want.

Moving along to the `Post List` we can see it is the same:

![API Post List screenshot]

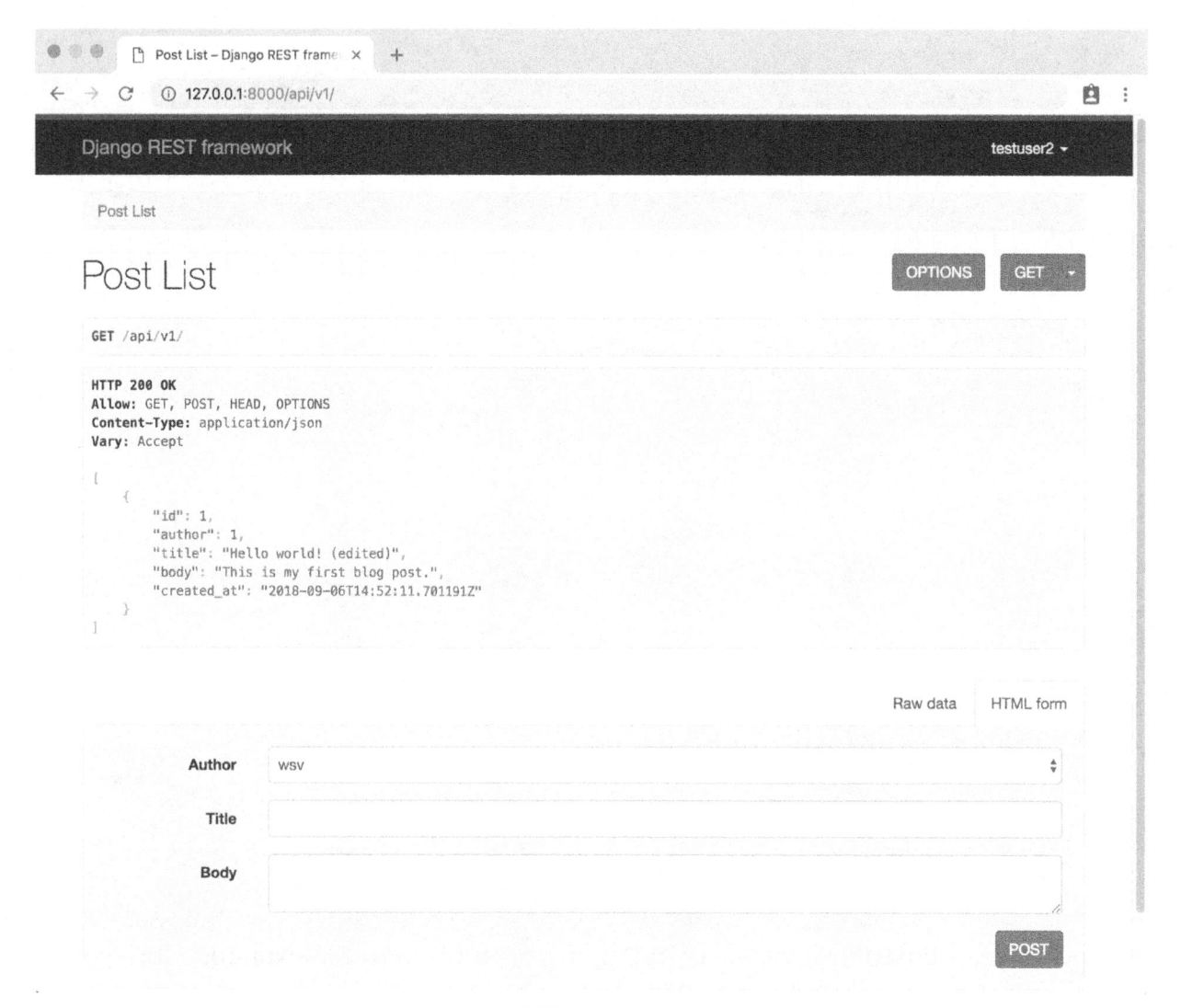

API Post List

And importantly our permissions still work. When logged-in with our `testuser2` account, the Post Instance is read-only.

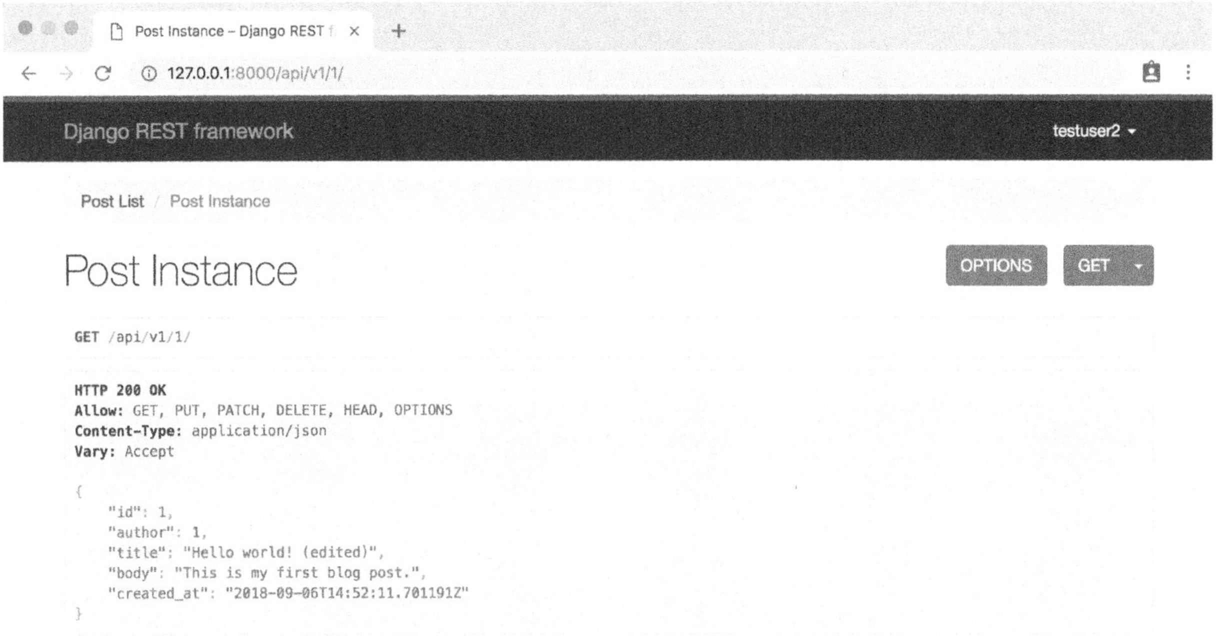
Post Instance – Django REST f
127.0.0.1:8000/api/v1/1/
Django REST framework
testuser2
Post List / Post Instance
Post Instance
OPTIONS
GET
GET /api/v1/1/
HTTP 200 OK
Allow: GET, PUT, PATCH, DELETE, HEAD, OPTIONS
Content-Type: application/json
Vary: Accept
{
"id": 1,
"author": 1,
"title": "Hello world! (edited)",
"body": "This is my first blog post.",
"created_at": "2018-09-06T14:52:11.701191Z"
}

API Post Instance Not Owner

However if we log in with our superuser account, which is the author of the solitary blog post, then we have full read-write-edit-delete privileges.

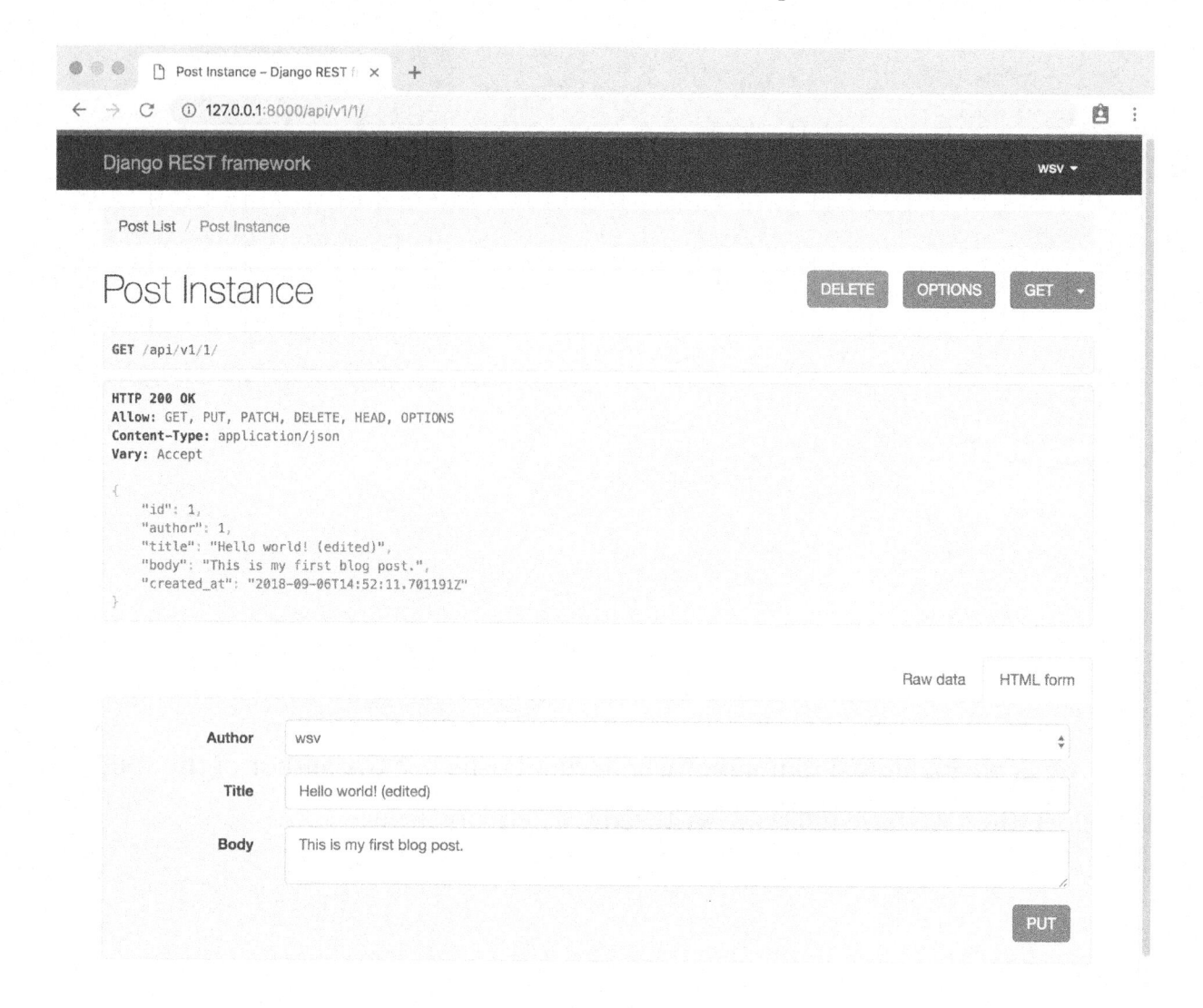

API Post Instance Owner

Conclusion

Viewsets and routers are a powerful abstraction that reduce the amount of code we as developers must write. However this conciseness comes at the cost of an initial learning curve. It will feel strange the first few times you use viewsets and routers instead of views and URL patterns.

Ultimately the decision of *when* to add viewsets and routers to your project is quite subjective. A good rule of thumb is to start with views and URLs. As your API grows in complexity if you find yourself repeating the same endpoint patterns over and over again, then look to viewsets and routers. Until then, keep things simple.

Chapter 9: Schemas and Documentation

Now that we have our API complete we need a way to document its functionality quickly and accurately to others. After all, in most companies and teams, the developer who is using the API is different from the developer who initially built it. Fortunately there are automated tools to handle this for us.

A schema is a machine-readable document that outlines all available API endpoints, URLs, and the HTTP verbs (GET, POST, PUT, DELETE, etc.) they support. Documentation is something added to a schema that makes it easier for humans to read and consume. In this chapter we will add a schema to our *Blog* project and then add two different documentation approaches. By the end we will we have implemented an automated way to document any current and future changes to our API.

As a reminder, here is the complete list of our current API endpoints:

Diagram

Endpoint	HTTP Verb
/	GET
/:pk/	GET
users/	GET
users/:pk/	GET
/rest-auth/registration	POST
/rest-auth/login	POST
/rest-auth/logout	GET
/rest-auth/password/reset	POST
/rest-auth/password/reset/confirm	POST

Schemas

Django REST Framework uses Core API[130] to provide an automatically generated API schema for us. Core API is format-independent which means it can be used in a wide variety of documentation. Basically you will usually use Core API as a first step to generate a schema, and *then* decide on which document format you want to use it in.

We also need to install pyyaml[131] which will let us render our schema in the commonly used YAML-based OpenAPI format.

Let's start by installing both packages. Make sure the local server is not running Control+c.

Command Line

```
(blogapi) $ pipenv install coreapi==2.3.3 pyyaml==3.13
```

Django REST Framework has built-in support for Core API so we just need to add it to our project-level `blog_project/urls.py` file. No advanced configuration required.

Here is the code.

---

[130]http://www.coreapi.org/
[131]https://pyyaml.org/

Code

```python
# blog_project/urls.py
from django.contrib import admin
from django.urls import include, path
from rest_framework.schemas import get_schema_view # new

schema_view = get_schema_view(title='Blog API') # new

urlpatterns = [
    path('admin/', admin.site.urls),
    path('api/v1/', include('posts.urls')),
    path('api-auth/', include('rest_framework.urls')),
    path('api/v1/rest-auth/', include('rest_auth.urls')),
    path('api/v1/rest-auth/registration/',
        include('rest_auth.registration.urls')),
    path('schema/', schema_view), # new
]
```

We import `get_schema_view` up top, give it the title `Blog API`, and then add a URL route for `schema/`. That's it!

If you start the local server again with `python manage.py runserver` and navigate to our new schema URL endpoint at http://127.0.0.1:8000/schema/[132] we can see an automatically generated schema of our entire API is available.

[132] http://127.0.0.1:8000/schema/

API Schema

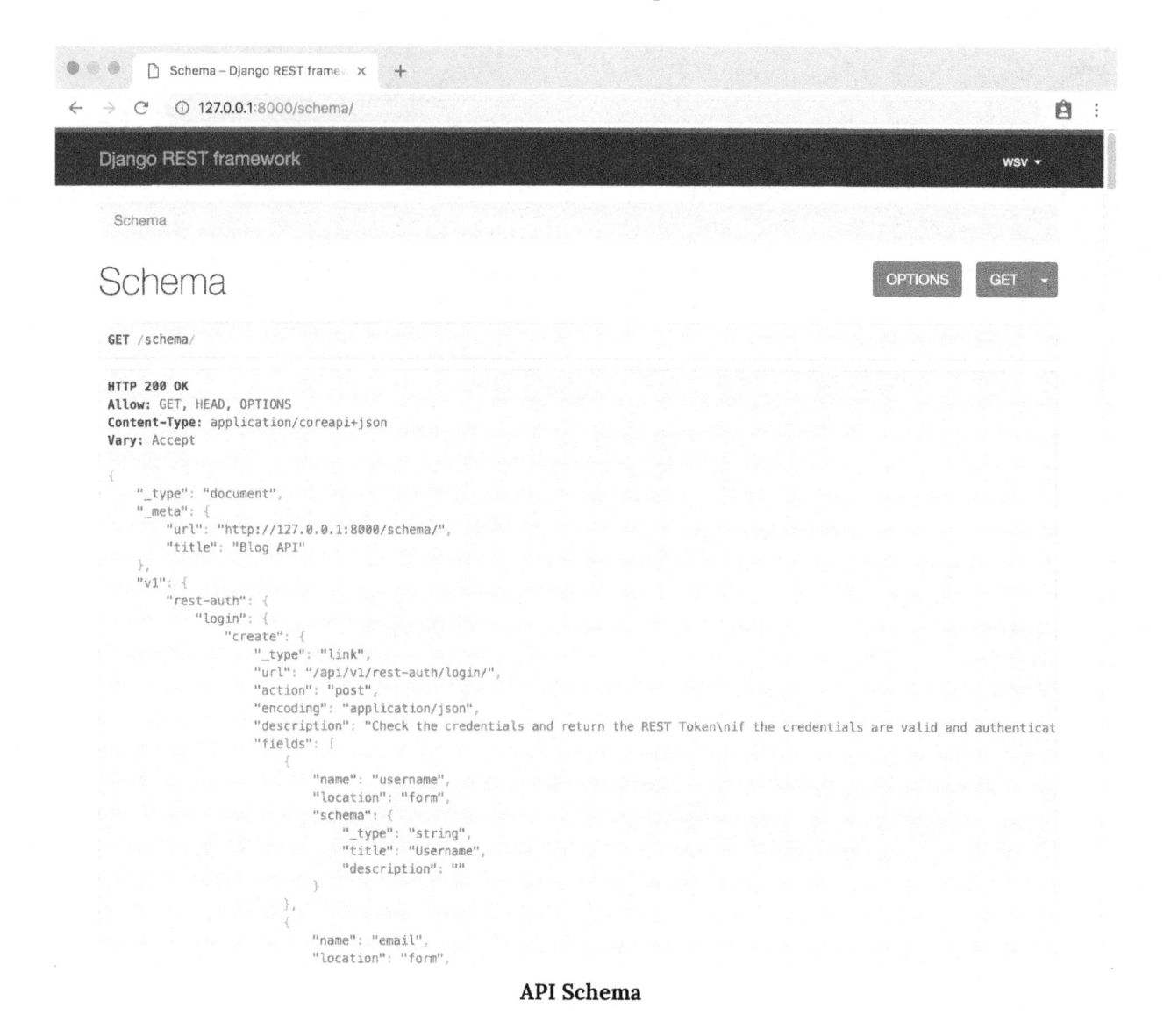

Documentation

Since a schema is designed for machines, not humans, to read Django REST Framework also comes with a built-in API documentation feature that translates schema into a *much* friendlier format for fellow developers.

To include the default API documentation we need to add two additional lines to our `urls.py` file. First import `include_docs_urls` and then add a new route for `docs/`.

Code

```
# blog_project/urls.py
from django.contrib import admin
from django.urls import include, path
from rest_framework.documentation import include_docs_urls # new
from rest_framework.schemas import get_schema_view

schema_view = get_schema_view(title='Blog API')

urlpatterns = [
    path('admin/', admin.site.urls),
    path('api/v1/', include('posts.urls')),
    path('api-auth/', include('rest_framework.urls')),
    path('api/v1/rest-auth/', include('rest_auth.urls')),
    path('api/v1/rest-auth/registration/',
        include('rest_auth.registration.urls')),
    path('docs/', include_docs_urls(title='Blog API')), # new
    path('schema/', schema_view),
]
```

That's it! Now navigate to the new route at http://127.0.0.1:8000/docs/[133] and you can see a much friendlier, visual view of our API.

---

[133]http://127.0.0.1:8000/docs/

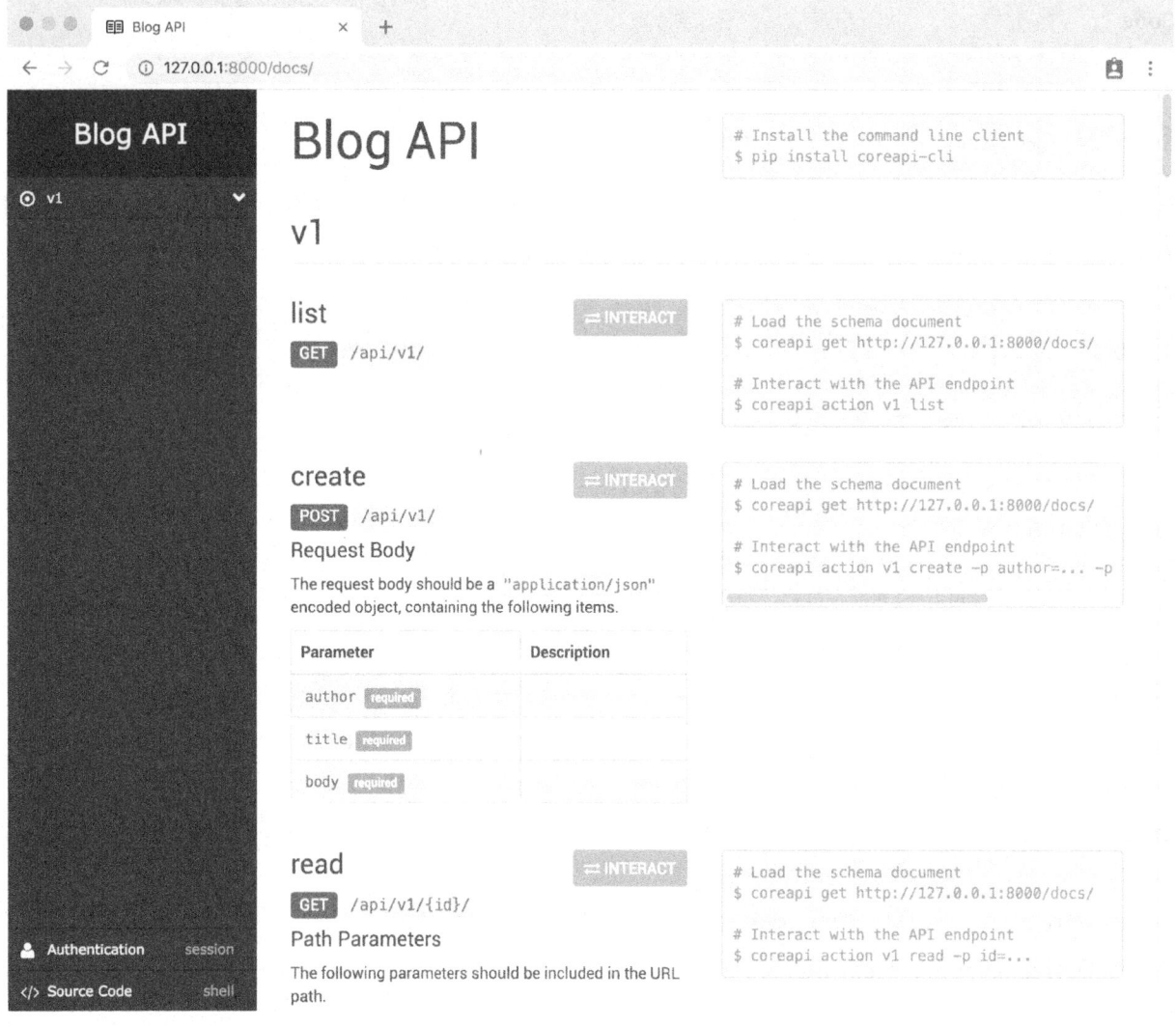

API Docs

As a small housekeeping manner, you may have noticed that we're repeating our title in the `urls.py` file. Since we always want to be as DRY[134] as possible let's add a variable `API_TITLE` for the API title instead. And while we're at it, let's add an API description for our docs too.

---
[134]https://en.wikipedia.org/wiki/Don%27t_repeat_yourself

Code

```python
# blog_project/urls.py
from django.contrib import admin
from django.urls import include, path
from rest_framework.documentation import include_docs_urls
from rest_framework.schemas import get_schema_view

API_TITLE = 'Blog API' # new
API_DESCRIPTION = 'A Web API for creating and editing blog posts.' # new
schema_view = get_schema_view(title=API_TITLE) # new

urlpatterns = [
    path('admin/', admin.site.urls),
    path('api/v1/', include('posts.urls')),
    path('api-auth/', include('rest_framework.urls')),
    path('api/v1/rest-auth/', include('rest_auth.urls')),
    path('api/v1/rest-auth/registration/',
        include('rest_auth.registration.urls')),
    path('docs/', include_docs_urls(title=API_TITLE,
                                    description=API_DESCRIPTION)), # new
    path('schema/', schema_view),
]
```

Much better. Now if you refresh our docs page you can see the description is present under our title.

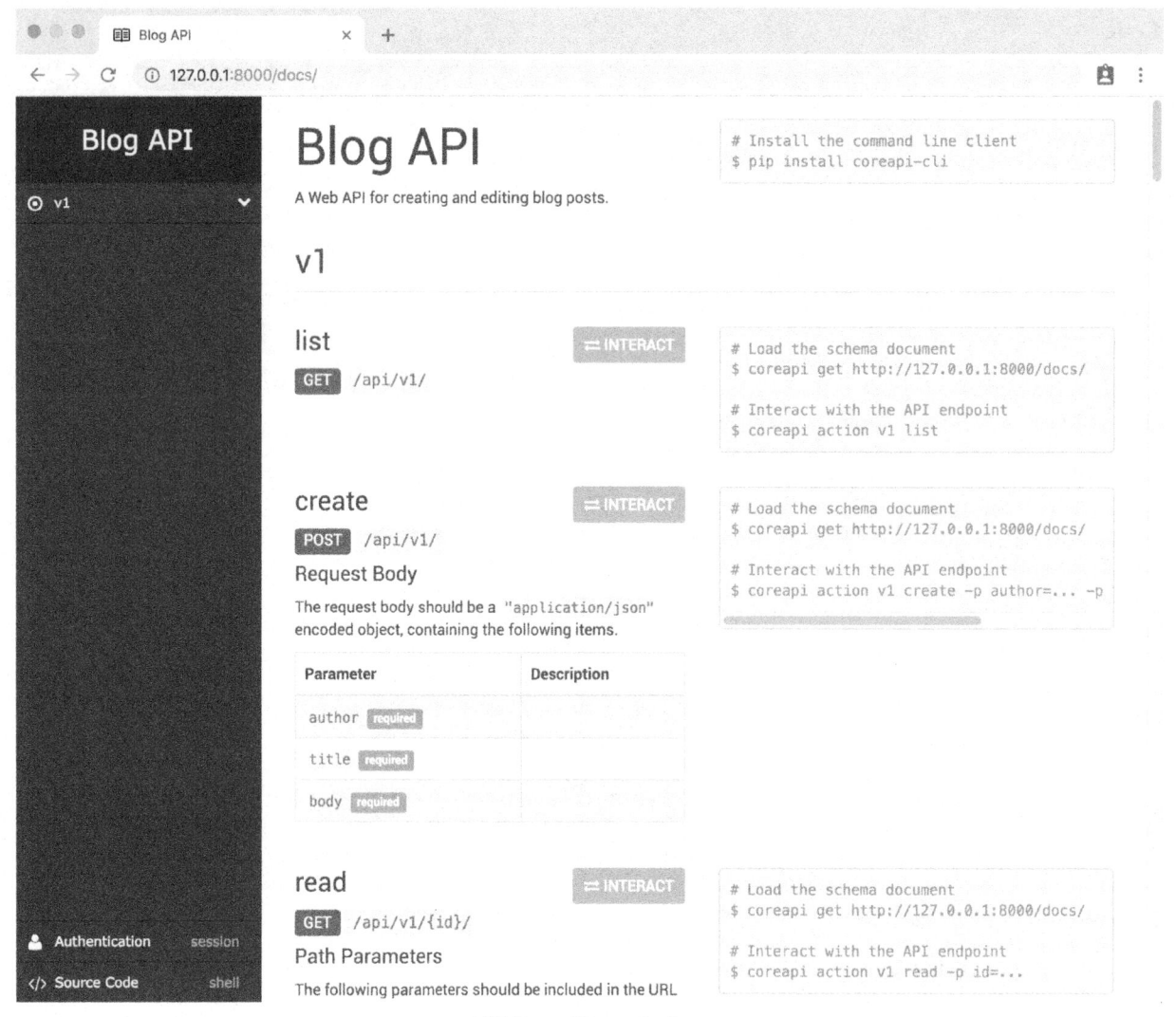

API Docs Description

We can also interact with this documentation in several ways. For example, try clicking on the "Interact" button next to `list` at the top of the page. A pop-up window will appear that is blank.

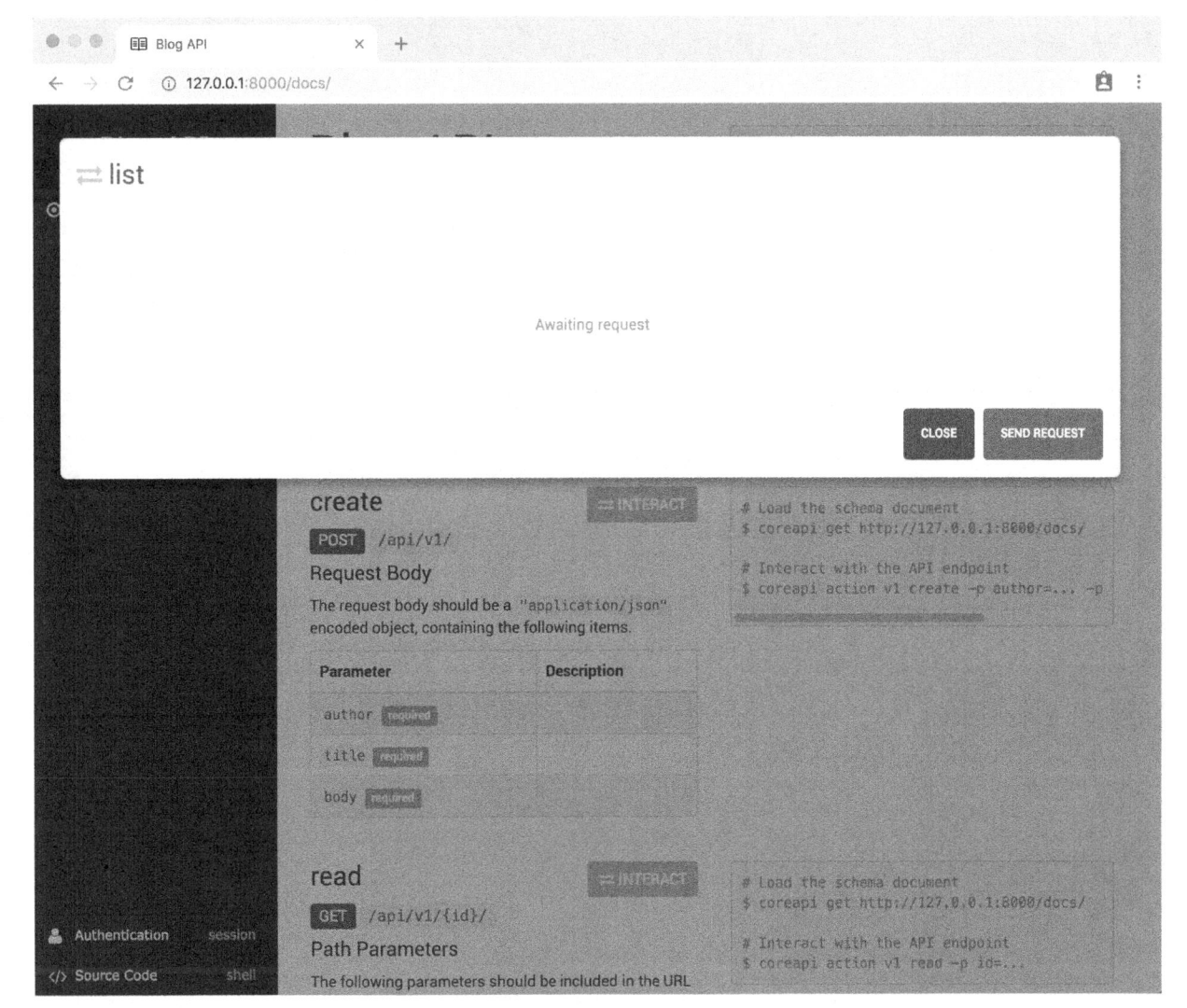

List Endpoint

Click on the button "SEND REQUEST" which will call the API endpoint.

180   Chapter 9: Schemas and Documentation

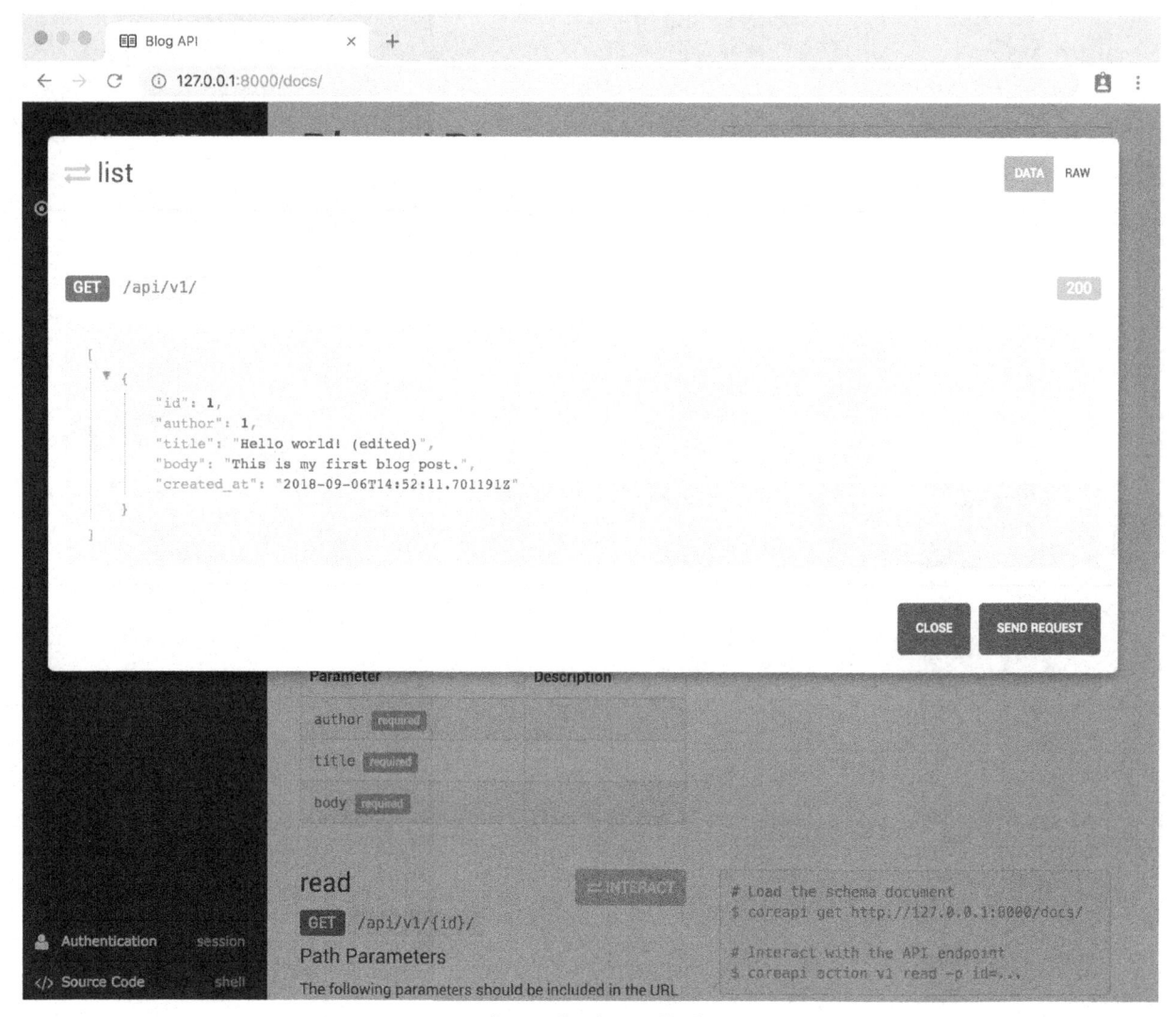

List Endpoint Called

In the same way we can interact with each of the other API endpoints available and fully documented.

Django REST Swagger

While the built-in Django REST Framework documentation is quite good, there is an even better way available. We can use the excellent third-party Django REST

Swagger[135] package to implement the OpenAPI Specification[136] with a tool called Swagger[137]. This is the current best-practice approach for documenting a RESTful API.

First stop the local server `Control+c`. Then install `django-rest-swagger` on the command line.

Command Line

```
(blogapi) $ pipenv install django-rest-swagger==2.2.0
```

Add it to our `INSTALLED_APPS` setting in `blog_project/settings.py` since it is a third-party app, not something with built-in support like `coreapi`.

Code

```
# blog_project/settings.py
INSTALLED_APPS = [
    'django.contrib.admin',
    'django.contrib.auth',
    'django.contrib.contenttypes',
    'django.contrib.sessions',
    'django.contrib.messages',
    'django.contrib.staticfiles',
    'django.contrib.sites',

    # 3rd-party apps
    'rest_framework',
    'rest_framework.authtoken',
    'rest_framework_swagger', # new
```

---

[135] https://marcgibbons.com/django-rest-swagger/
[136] https://swagger.io/resources/open-api/
[137] https://swagger.io/

```
    'allauth',
    'allauth.account',
    'allauth.socialaccount',
    'rest_auth',
    'rest_auth.registration',

    # Local
    'posts.apps.PostsConfig',
]
```

Finally we want to replace the default schema with our new Swagger schema in `blog_project/urls.py`. Import `get_swagger_view` at the top of the file. Update the `schema_view` to use Swagger now, so `get_swagger_view` not the previous `get_schema_view`. And comment out the old route for `schema/`, adding a new one for `swagger-docs`.

Code

```
# blog_project/urls.py
from django.contrib import admin
from django.urls import include, path
from rest_framework.documentation import include_docs_urls
from rest_framework.schemas import get_schema_view
from rest_framework_swagger.views import get_swagger_view # new

API_TITLE = 'Blog API'
API_DESCRIPTION = 'A Web API for creating and editing blog posts.'
schema_view = get_swagger_view(title=API_TITLE) # new

urlpatterns = [
    path('admin/', admin.site.urls),
```

```
    path('api/v1/', include('posts.urls')),
    path('api-auth/', include('rest_framework.urls')),
    path('docs/', include_docs_urls(title=API_TITLE,
                            description=API_DESCRIPTION)),
    # path('schema/', schema_view), # new
    path('swagger-docs/', schema_view), # new
]
```

Make sure the server is running (`python manage.py runserver`) navigate to the new Swagger route at http://127.0.0.1:8000/swagger-docs/[138] you'll see the result.

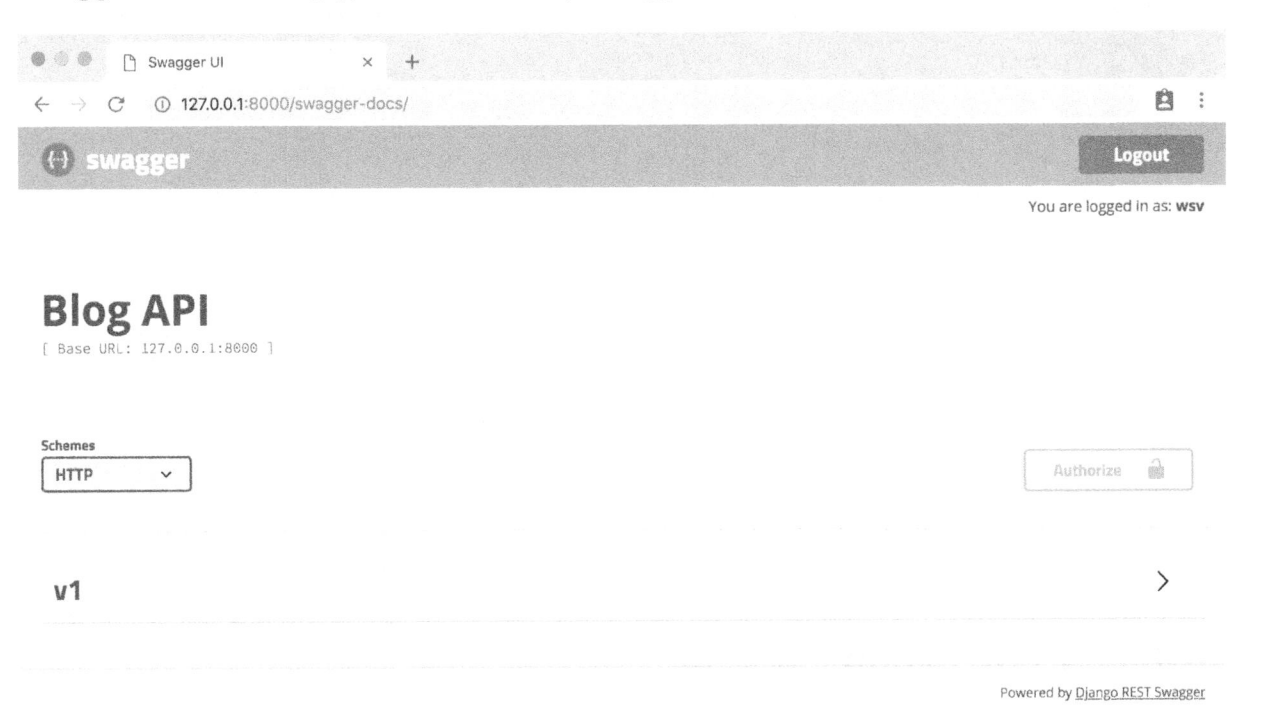

API Swagger Documentation

But where's the data you may be asking? Click on `v1` to expose a dropdown list of all the supported endpoints and HTTP methods available.

---
[138]http://127.0.0.1:8000/swagger-docs/

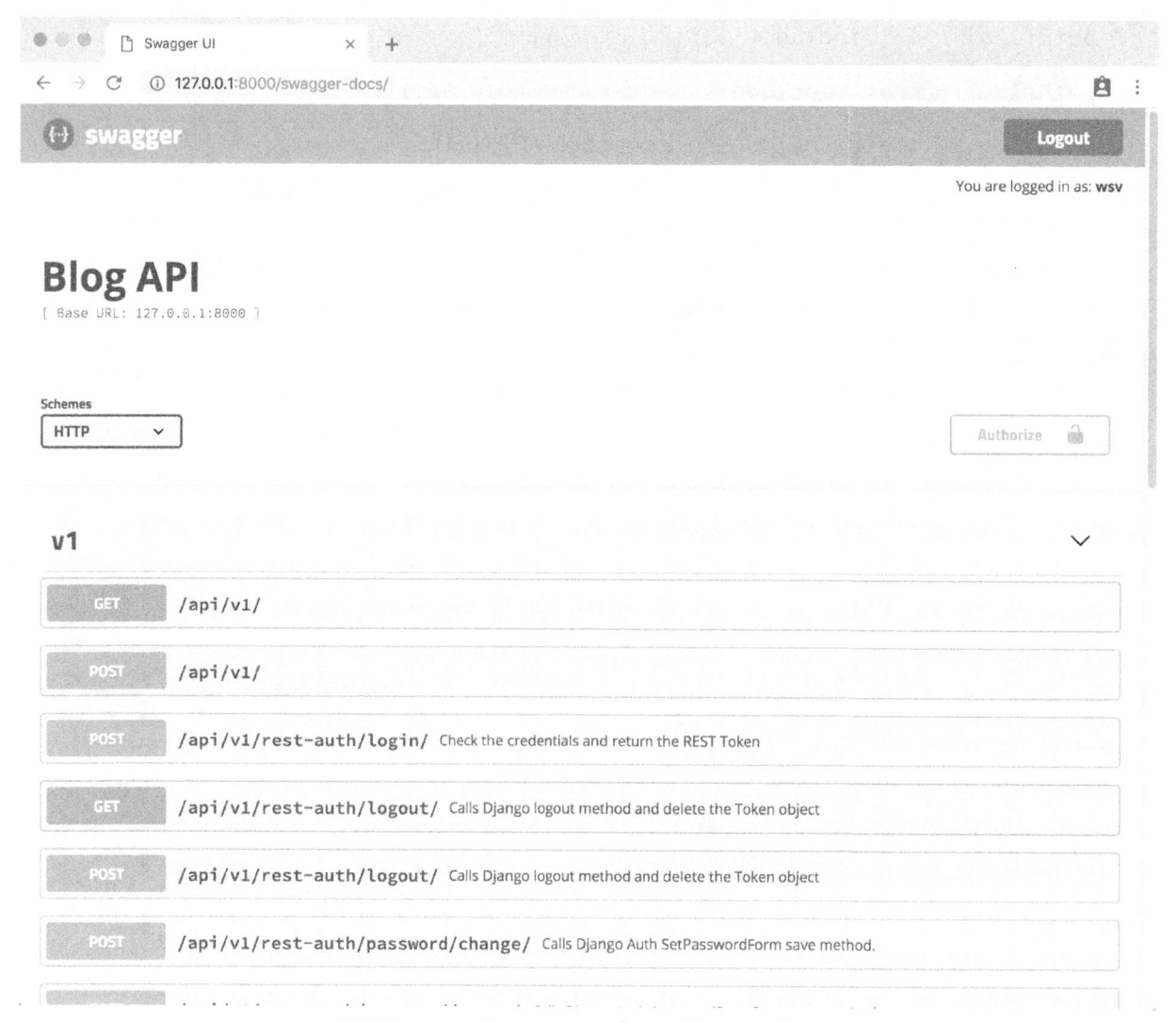

API Swagger Documentation with Dropdown

Swagger Log In and Log Out

There are a number of ways to customize Swagger which can be found in the official documentation[139]. One additional setting that we should update is log in and log out. If you tried previously to click on the "Session Login" button in the upper right corner it doesn't work. We need to specify the correct log in and log out routes.

At the bottom of the `blog_project/settings.py` file, add the following Swagger set-

---
[139]https://django-rest-swagger.readthedocs.io/en/latest/settings/

tings.

Code

```
# blog_project/settings.py
SWAGGER_SETTINGS = {
    'LOGIN_URL': 'rest_framework:login',
    'LOGOUT_URL': 'rest_framework:logout',
}
```

That's it! The "Login Session" and "Logout" buttons will now work correctly.

Conclusion

Adding documentation is a vital part of any API. It is typically the first thing a fellow developer looks at, either within a team or on an open-source projects. Thanks to the automated tools covered in this chapter, ensuring your API has accurate, up-to-date documentation only requires a small amount of configuration.

Conclusion

We're now at the end of the book but only the beginning of what can be accomplished with Django REST Framework. Over the course of three different projects–*Library* API, *Todo* API, and *Blog* API–we have built progressively more complex web APIs from scratch. And it's no accident that at every step along the way, Django REST Framework provides built-in features to make our life easier.

If you've never built web APIs before with another framework be forewarned that you've been spoiled. And if you have, rest assured this book only scratches the surface of what Django REST Framework can do. The official documentation[140] is an excellent resource for further exploration now that you have a handle on the basics.

Next Steps

The biggest area worthy of further exploration is testing. Traditional Django tests can and should be applied to any web API project, but there is also a whole suite[141] of tools in Django REST Framework just for testing API requests.

A good next step is to implement the pastebin API covered in official tutorial[142]. I've even written an updated beginners guide[143] guide to it that features step-by-step instructions.

Third-party packages are as essential to Django REST Framework development as they are to Django itself. A complete listing can be found at Django Packages[144] or a

---

[140] http://www.django-rest-framework.org/
[141] http://www.django-rest-framework.org/api-guide/testing/
[142] http://www.django-rest-framework.org/tutorial/1-serialization/
[143] https://wsvincent.com/official-django-rest-framework-tutorial-beginners-guide/
[144] https://djangopackages.org/

curated list on the awesome-django[145] repo on Github.

Giving Thanks

While the Django community is quite large and relies on the hard work of many individuals, Django REST Framework is much smaller in comparison. It was initially created by Tom Christie[146], an English software engineer who now works on it full-time thanks to open-source funding. He still leads active development. If you enjoy working with Django REST Framework, please consider taking a moment to personally thank him on Twitter[147].

And thank **you** for reading along and supporting my work. If you have any feedback I can be reached at will@wsvincent.com[148].

---

[145] https://github.com/wsvincent/awesome-django
[146] http://www.tomchristie.com/
[147] https://twitter.com/_tomchristie
[148] mailto:will@wsvincent.com

Acknowledgements

Thank you to the following developers who read early versions of this manuscript and provided help and encouragement throughout the writing process:

- Tom Christie
- Angel Crujiff
- Vitor Freitas
- Daniel Roy Greenfeld
- Michael Herman
- Chandler Lutz
- Victor L.
- Richard Mace
- José Padilla
- Jeff Triplett

Made in the USA
Columbia, SC
30 November 2018